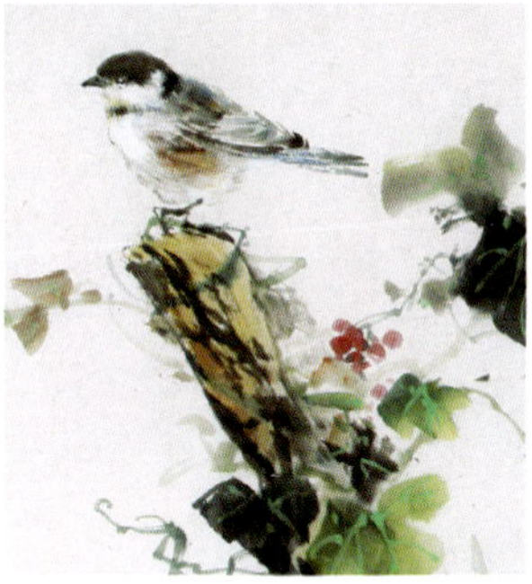

DISCOVER THE ARTIST WITHIN YOU

CHINESE BRUSH PAINTING

THE EASY WAY

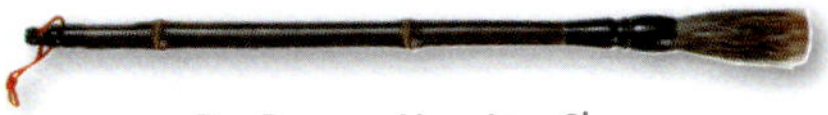

By Danny Han-Lin Chen

This edition published in 2012
by SpiceBox™
12171 Horseshoe Way,
Richmond, BC,
Canada V7A 4V4

First published in 2007

ISBN 10: 1-927010-09-8
ISBN 13: 978-1-927010-09-9

CEO and Publisher: Ben Lotfi
Author/Artist: Danny Chen
Editor: Trisha Pope
Creative Director: Garett Chan
Art Director: Christine Covert
Designer: Morgen Price, Charmaine Muzyka
Production: James Badger
Photographer: James Badger
Sourcing: Janny Lam

For more SpiceBox products and information, visit our website:
www.spicebox.ca

Manufactured in China

3 5 7 9 10 8 6 4

TABLE OF CONTENTS

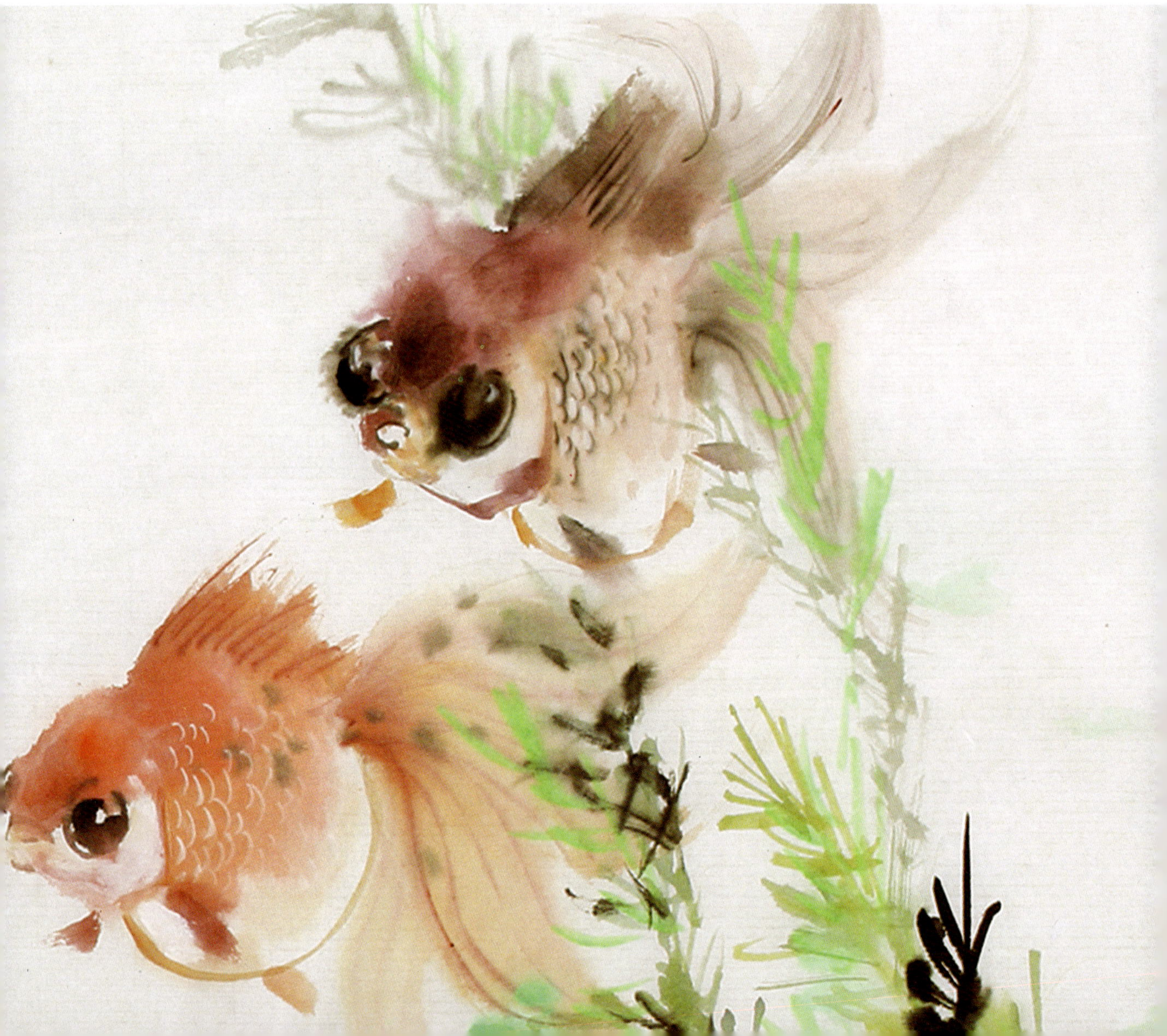

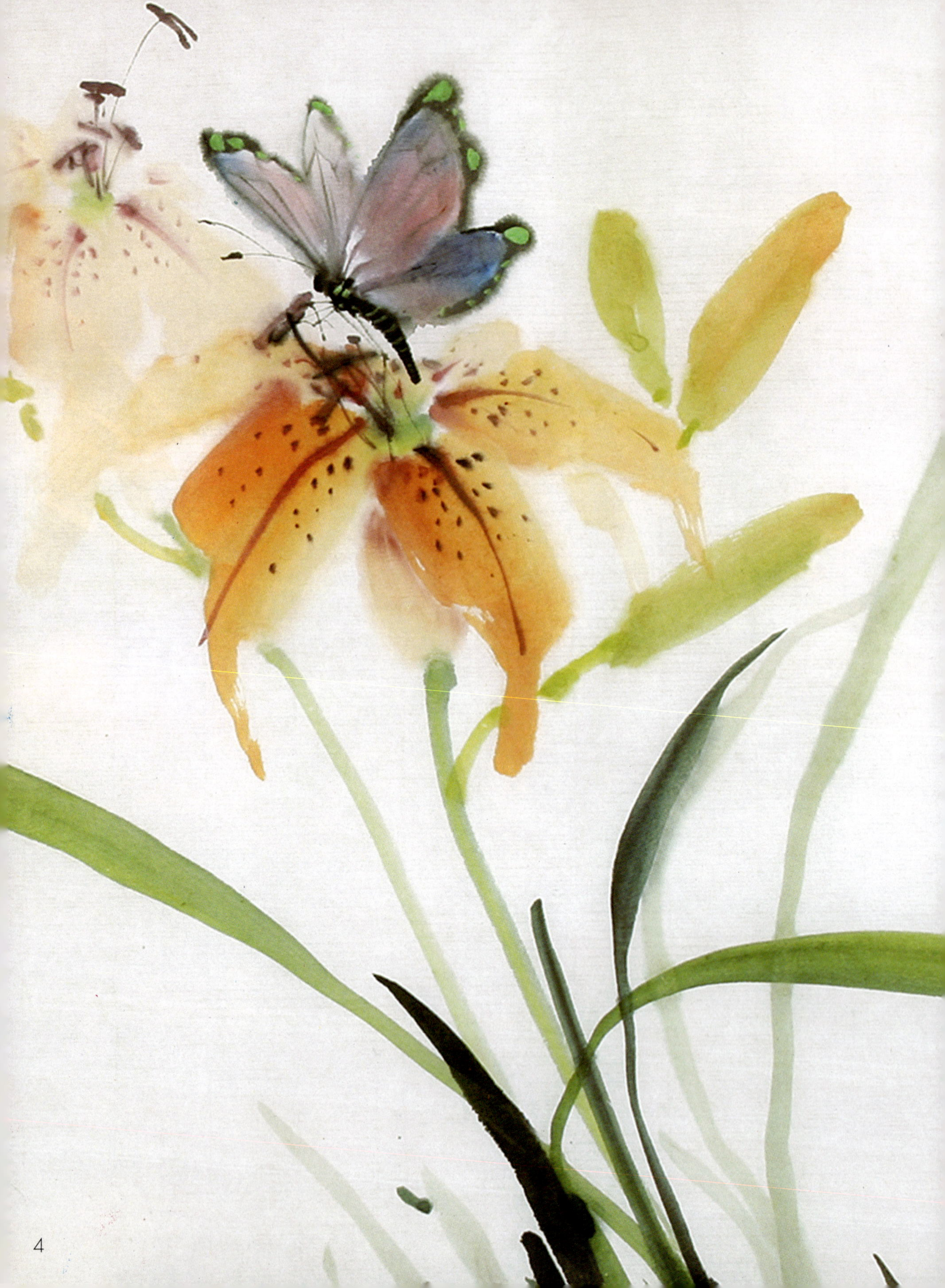

Introduction — Harmonious Space

Over my many years of teaching and in my own artist's statement, I have said that to paint is to create a harmonious balance of space — within and beyond the canvas. This holds especially true for Chinese painting, where the relative technical simplicity of the art belies the sensitivity and sensibility for composition that develops over time. Indeed, in my nearly twenty-five years of experience as an art instructor, I have seen that Chinese painting is remarkably easy to learn and satisfying to do, but is also difficult to master. In this book, I'll show you the techniques I've used and taught over many years — techniques that are tried and proven, and will, with practice and dedication, result in the ability to render an array of traditional and non-traditional subjects.

I started to study art at a very young age. At first, I concentrated on watercolor and oils — honing my own skills through hours of devoted practice. My various instructors encouraged me early on, by entering my works in competitions in Taiwan, Japan, Korea, Germany, the United States and Canada. My success at this level of competition encouraged me even further and after moving to Canada, I eventually became a member of the Federation of Canadian Artists in 1984 and attained my signature member status (A.F.C.A). Today my work continues to receive recognition in Canada and abroad.

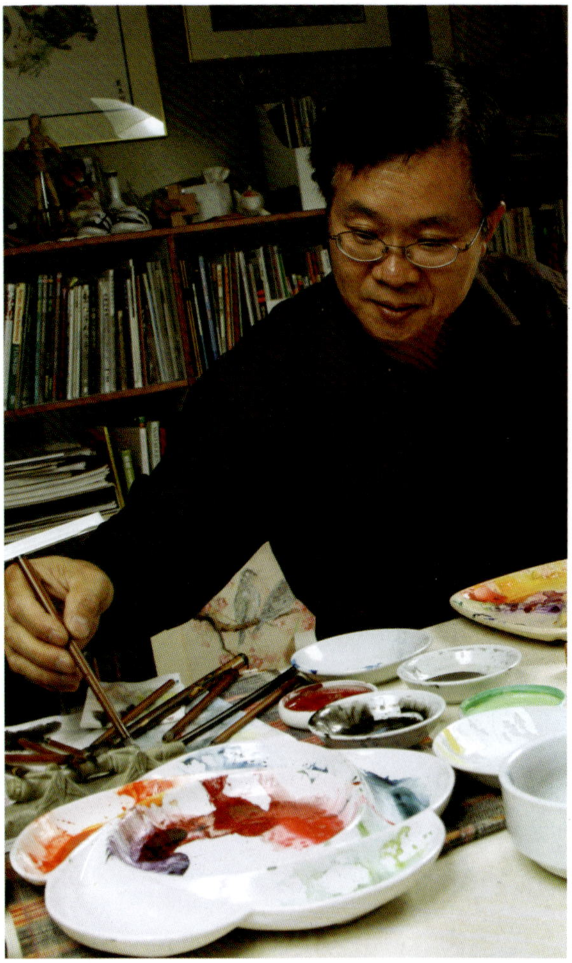

ABOVE: Artist and Teacher Danny Han-Lin Chen

All of which is to say that art plays a fundamental role in my life and has enriched me deeply. Art is a gift. It provides the artist with greater perspective and sensitivity, and what is more, it provides the viewer of an artwork the joy of seeing through another person's eyes. I firmly believe the value of an artwork is in the experience of creating the work of art, experiencing the world through touch, sight and feeling. I believe that the result is secondary to the experience of making art, and one of the best places to begin is with the rich art of Chinese brush painting — an art that traces back thousands of years. Since then, many styles have developed and traditions have been established. For my part, I try to teach and practice a reverence for tradition, while attempting to evolve it further. At the same time, I try to maintain the central characteristic of the form, that being a close observance of nature and a reliance on spontaneity. Early on in the history of Chinese painting, a style arose that roughly translated means "throwing paint" — and that is what I have tried to underline and encourage in my classes. I wish for my students to develop a style of painting that depends on sight and inspiration, while balancing the composition with the natural world around it.

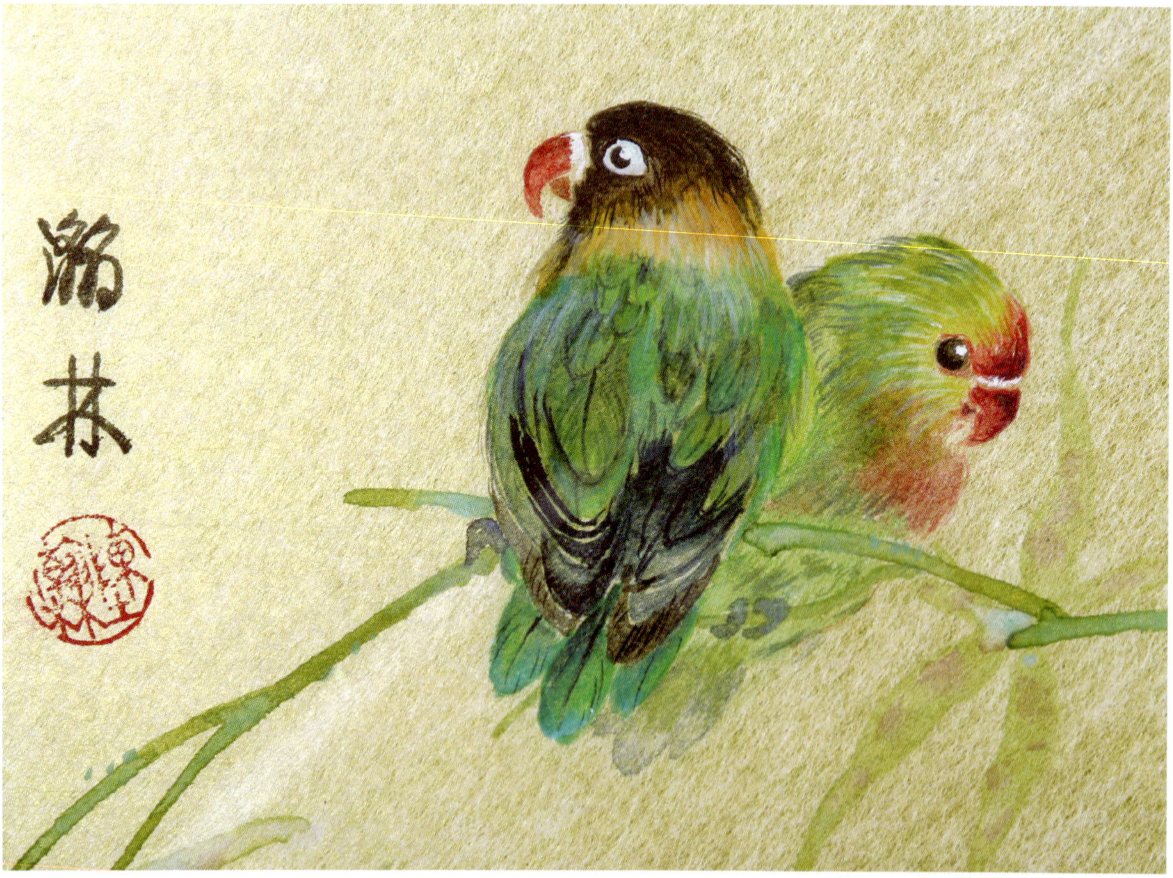

Materials

At the start of any journey to master a new art form, you need to learn how to use materials inherent to that discipline. In the case of Chinese painting, there are a few differences from the materials used in Western watercolor painting. First, let's look at the basic supplies that come with this kit, as well as a few ancillary items you may wish to have.

A) **White Cloud Brush:** used for painting soft objects, petals, some types of leaves and filling color.

B) **Orchid Bamboo Brush:** A larger brush used for heavier objects; tree trunks, large grasses and bamboo, some types of petals and leaves.

C) **Vine Brush:** A small, detail brush used for more delicate items, outlining, thin stems, stamens, antennae, eyes, and so forth.

D) **Ink Stick:** This is the compressed, dried ink that you will grind to make concentrated liquid ink.

E) **Ink Stone:** This is what you grind the dried ink on with a few drops of water to make concentrated liquid ink.

F) **Brush Rest:** You do not want to leave your brushes standing in water. When not in use, rest them on this stand.

G) **Chinese Watercolor Paints:** You will use these in a similar manner to Western watercolor paints, however, traditional watercolors do not bind to the paper as well when you stretch it, so do not use them for work you wish to display. Only use Chinese colors.

H) **Blanket or Pad:** You will use this under your paper and is explained in more detail in the following pages.

I) **Ceramic dishes:** White ceramic dishes work well for holding your ink and paints. You could also use a watercolor palette.

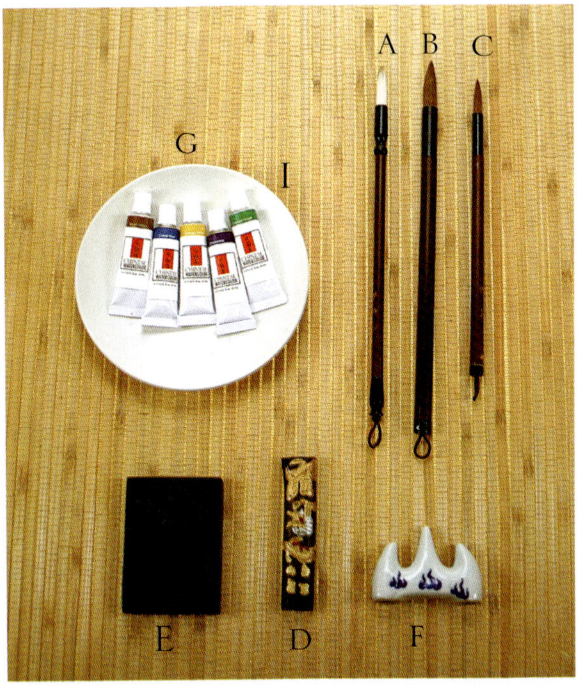

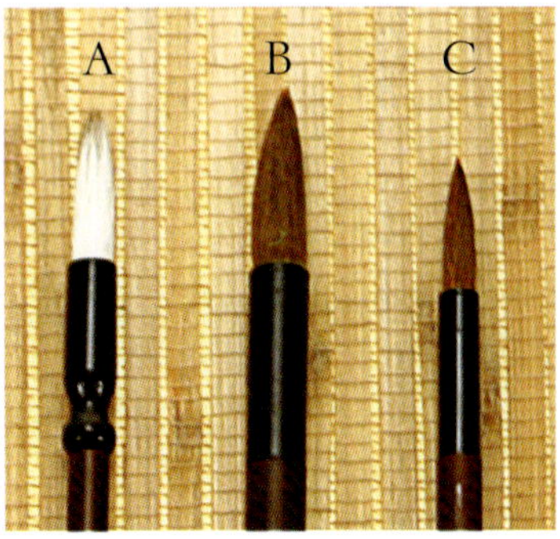

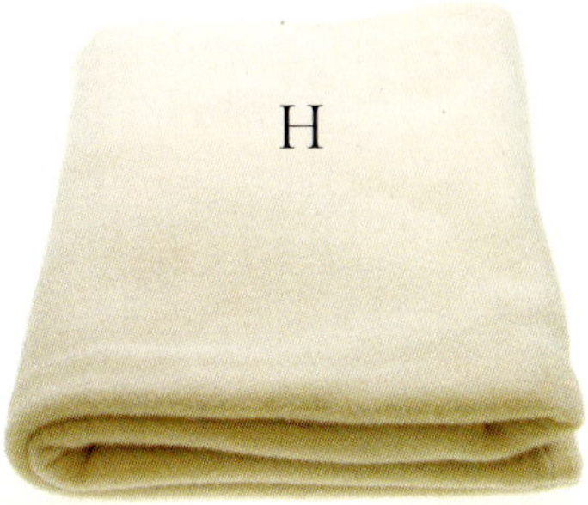

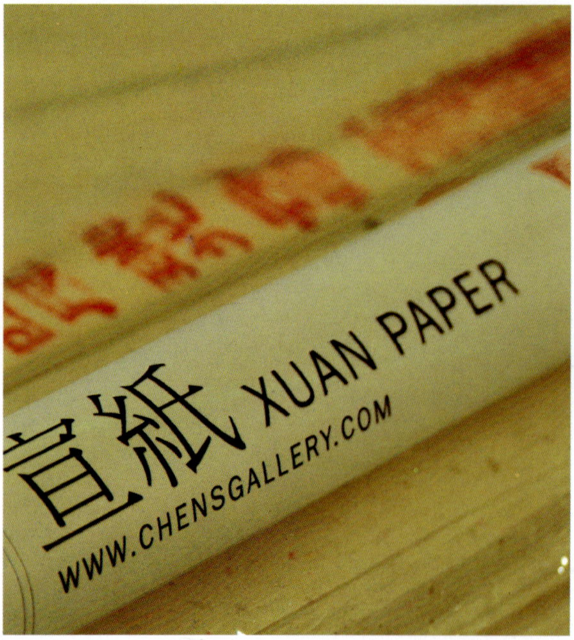

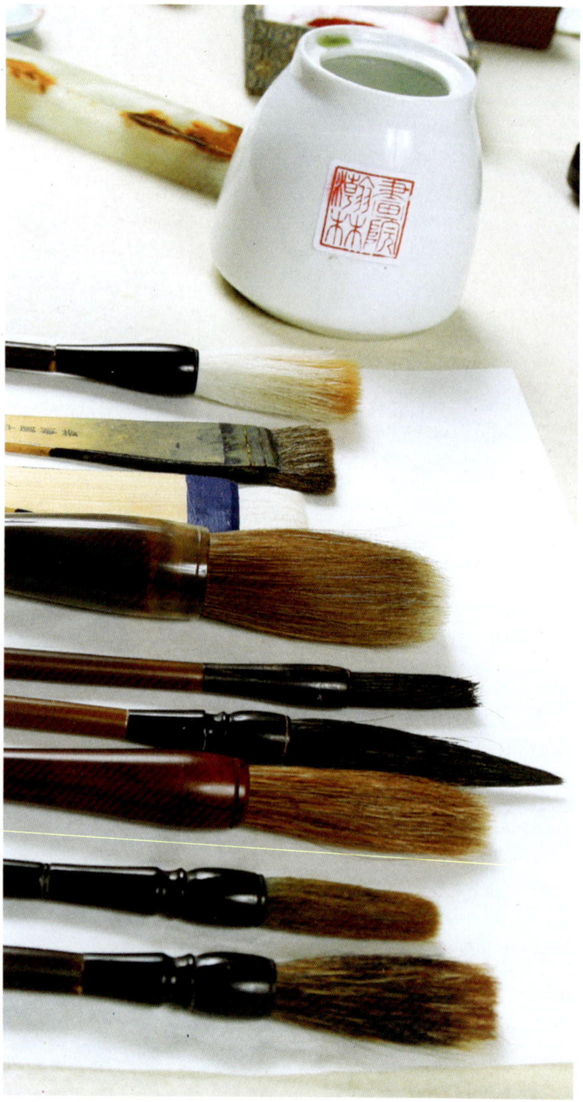

ABOVE: Soft brushes are made from goat hair, sable, or synthetic fibre. Harder brushes are made from horse hair, or boar hair.

Paper

The best paper to achieve optimal results is Chinese Xuan Paper, a type of rice paper. This paper is untreated, absorbent and works well when working spontaneously as I demonstrate throughout this book. There are other kinds of paper commonly used in Chinese painting in different degrees of absorbency. At the one end of the spectrum there are papers like xuan paper with high absorbency. At the other end of the spectrum there are alum-treated and other treated papers with very low levels of absorbency. There are a myriad of other papers in between that you may wish to experiment with at a later time; mulberry, for example is a popular option. To begin, however, there are ways to treat ordinary xuan paper to lower its absorbency if required so I recommend starting with this traditional paper and then applying this technique if required.

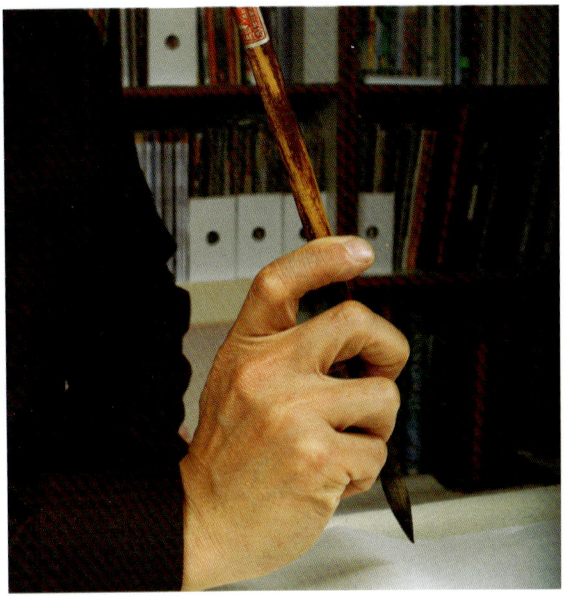

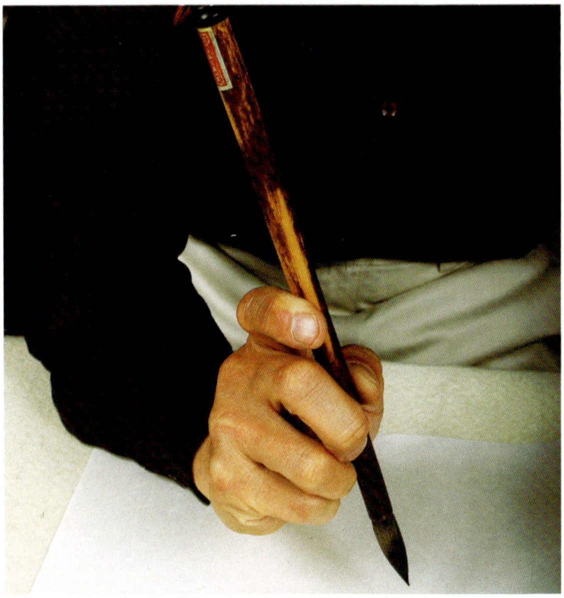

ABOVE: In this grip, the brush locks between your index and ring finger. This is the optimal position for painting details, or doing smaller strokes. Hold the brush at the top, between the thumb and forefinger when you want less control, and want to make broader, less refined strokes.

Brushes

Chinese brushes come with different kinds of bristles, normally from different animal fur or hair, but synthetic bristles are also becoming more commonly available. Each type of bristle has different absorbency characteristics and allows varying control over the paint. As a rule of thumb, brushes are classified as "hard" or "soft", and you would use them according to the subject you wish to paint. For instance, if you want to paint a soft subject, you may try a softer brush first, and when painting a hard object you would choose a hard bristle brush. Coarse bristles are also good for painting dry brush strokes for texture and woody objects like branches.

After you have used a brush, it is very important to clean the bristles by rinsing it in clear water just as you would with any other type of brush.

Keep a clean supply of water at hand, and at the end of your painting session, clean your brushes thoroughly and hang them so that any excess water or pigment makes its way down the bristles to the tip.

Once you have your brushes, the next step is learning the proper way to grip your brush. Each artist is free to find their own way, but the grip that I illustrate is very common and is a good place to begin handling a brush and ink. Where you grip the handle of the brush will depend on the flow of energy you wish to portray through your stroke. For more sweeping or loose brush strokes, hold the brush high on the handle. For tight, detailed or "hard" strokes, hold the brush lower down on the handle, closer to the bristles.

Strokes

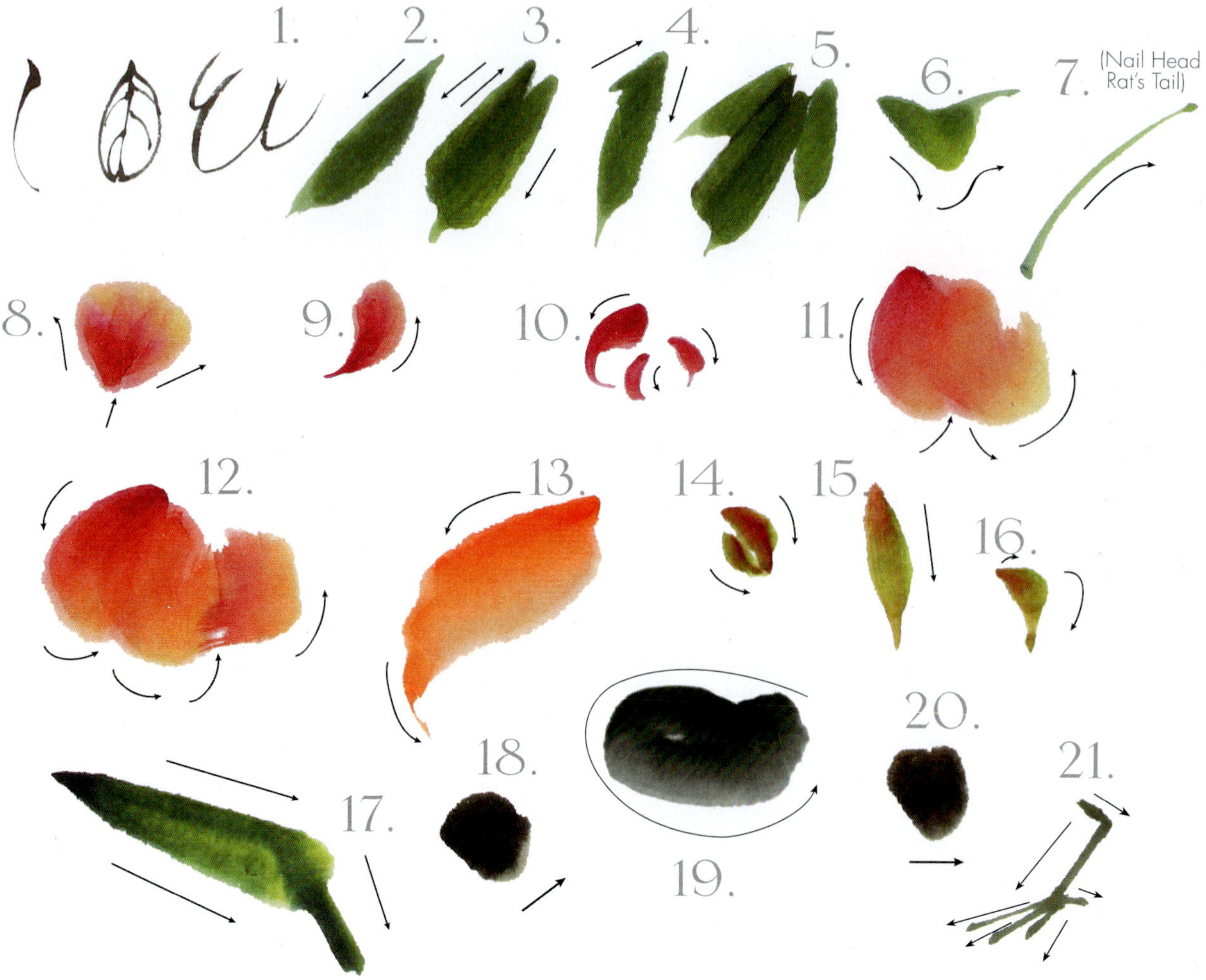

Strokes

Traditional Chinese brush painting uses a number of brush strokes that create the foundation for all painting and a student would master these basic strokes until they are perfected, before attempting compositions. I show them here and do refer to many of them that are used in the demonstrations in this book. In addition, samples 18 through 21 show stroke combinations and variations used to create the baby chicks in demonstration four. Having explained this, I have modified or adapted many of these traditional strokes to suit my style of painting, and encourage my students to paint right away, developing skills and personal style as they practice.

Basic Brush Loading Technique

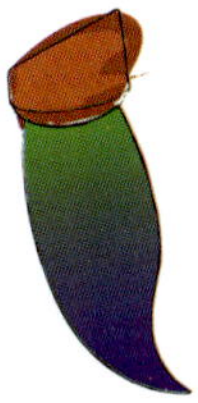

Fully loaded green with indigo halfway

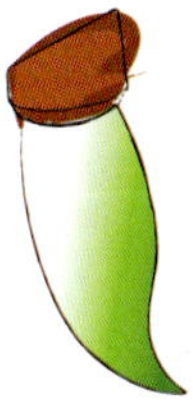

Fully loaded white with green halfway on one side only

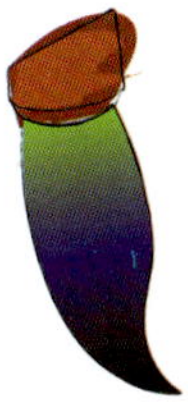

Fully loaded medium green with indigo halfway, and dark ink at the tip

Brush Loading

One important part of Chinese brush painting that must be mastered early on to achieve the richness and subtlety with this art, is the ability to load multiple colors onto your brush at one time, and control how these colors flow from the brush to the paper. The important thing to remember is that the first color is the base color and is fully loaded onto the bristles of the brush. The second color is an accent color, and you will load it until you see that it has been absorbed halfway up the bristles. The third color is also an accent and usually is quite a bit darker than the first two colors. Only the tip of the brush is dipped in this color. It will bleed off the bristles first as you paint your stroke, and only the second and first colors will show in the remainder of your stroke.

A technique I have developed in loading color is to load your second color on one side of the brush only. By doing this, and then flipping your brush over so the second color you load is on the top side of the brush, it will bleed through the sides of the bristles and create a subtle shading on both sides of the base color.

Painting Surface

Finally the last important detail that bears mentioning is that you must paint with a towel or small blanket placed underneath your paper in order for the paper to have the proper buoyancy or "bounce-back" against the force of your brush. You will also feel freer to make strokes that continue on past the edge of the paper. Also, from a more technical point of view, because rice paper is thin and absorbent, the water from your paint will soak through the paper quite easily. Without the towel underneath, your paper will become "glued" to the table by the water, and likely shred as you are painting.

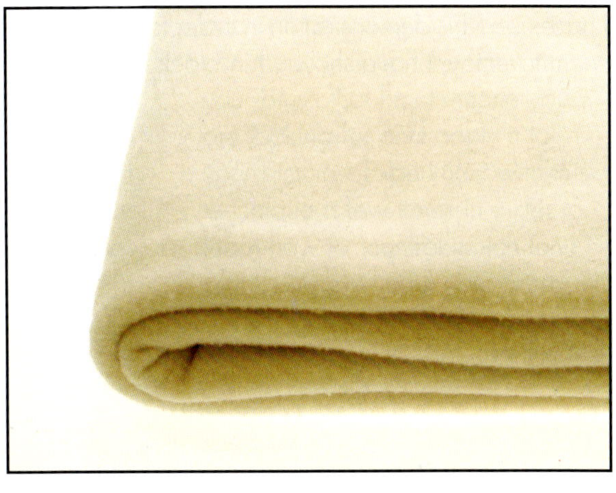

4.

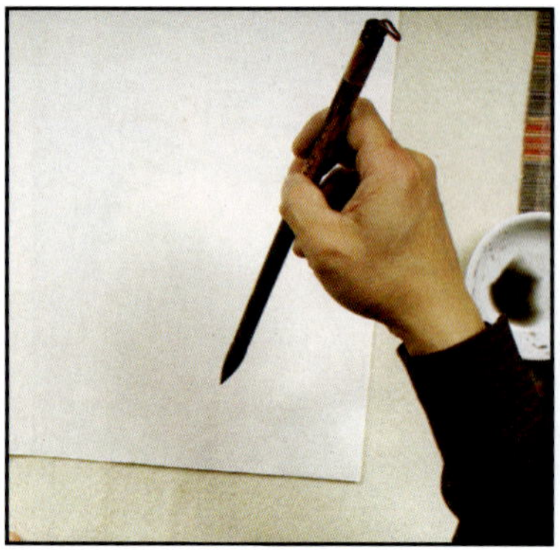

Let's start painting! Load the Orchid Bamboo brush with medium ink, and at the tip, pick up concentrated black ink. Holding the brush high on the handle with the bristles pointing to the bottom of your paper, make one continuous sweeping stroke, moving upwards from the base of your page to top right of the page. In this case, you want to apply pressure through the middle of the stroke, laying off at the beginning and end of the stroke to create the leaf typical of a cymbidium orchid.

5.

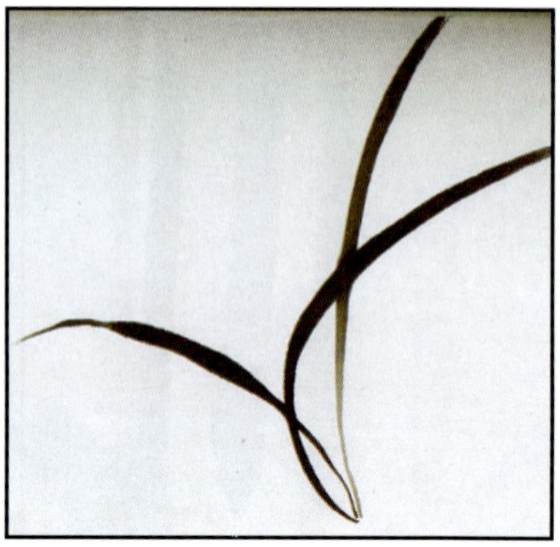

A hallmark of Chinese brush painting is controlling the absorption of the paper by applying more or less pressure with the brush. Practice varying your brush pressure as you make two more of these stems. Transverse one stroke with another at the bottom of your page to create an "eye" with the stems.

6.

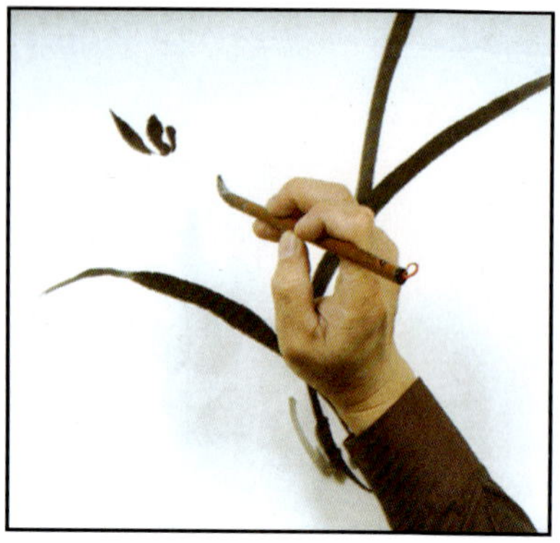

In addition, through practice, you will develop what we call "chi", which to the Chinese means "internal energy". Your personal chi translates through your body, into the brush and then finally releases into the strokes you produce to give a sense of energy and life to your orchid.

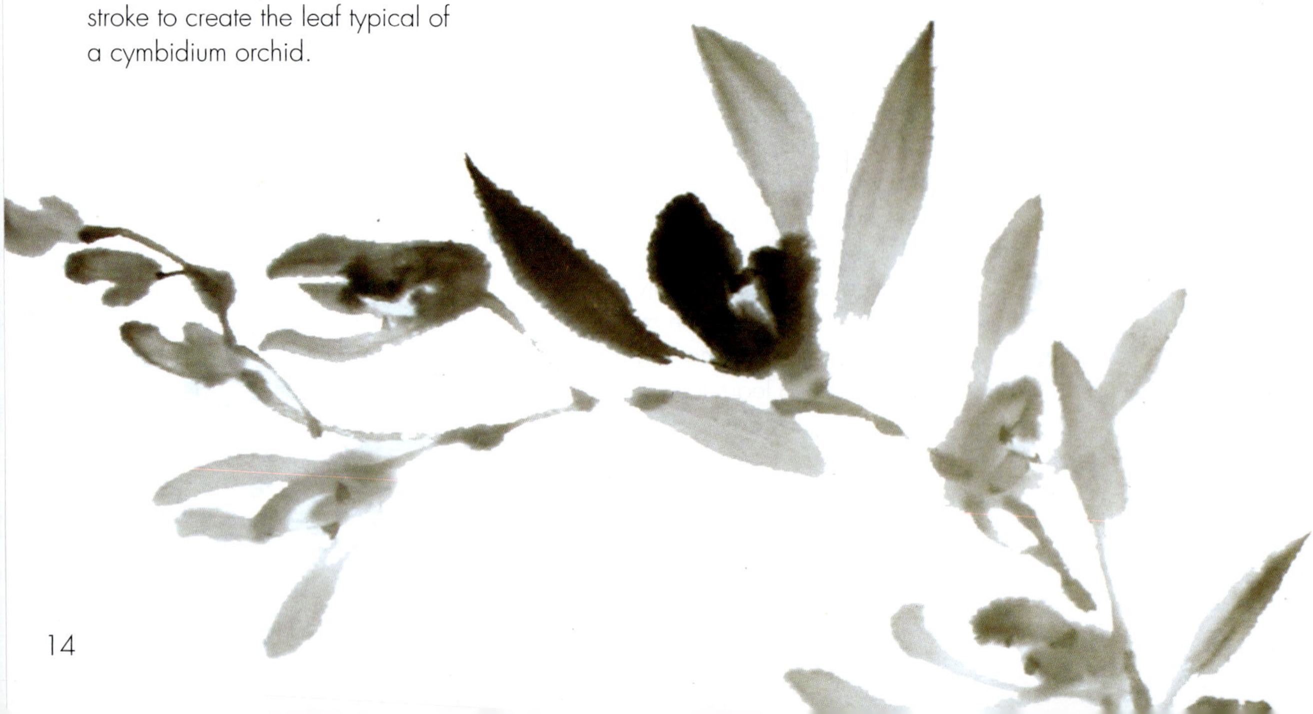

7.

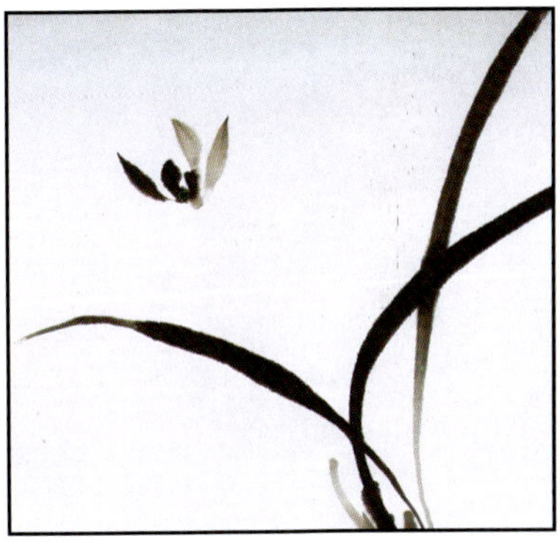

Refer to the chart on page 10 to practice strokes 14, 15 and 16. This group of strokes is the one we use to create the orchid flowers. Load your White Cloud brush with concentrated ink and use stroke 14 to create little buds with simple downward strokes. Add the larger petals with strokes 15 and 16.

8.

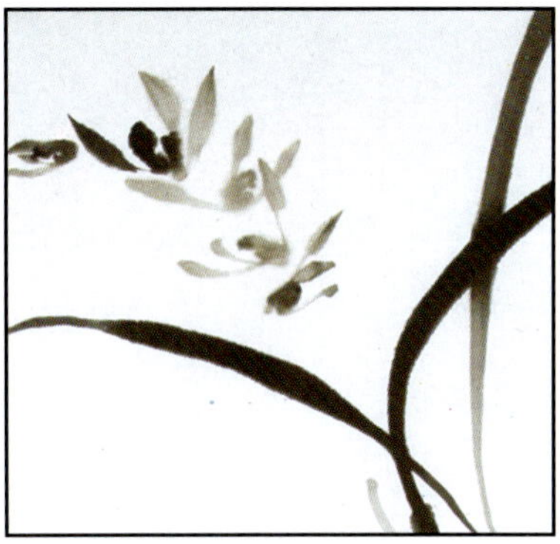

Without reloading your brush, add more petals near your first flower, and down the "stem" of the flower. You will notice that as the tone of your ink lightens, you create the appearance of depth in your composition. The lighter flowers appear to recede and the darker flowers appear to be forward. Reload your brush and add a few more buds and flowers to your spray.

9.

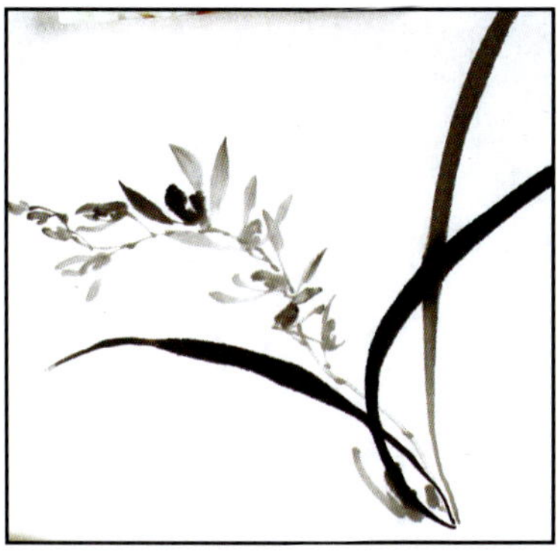

To finish the orchid, use your Vine brush to practice stroke 7 on page 10. You will use a series of these strokes to paint in the stem that the buds and flowers will join. Start at the top of the flowers and paint in the stem in to create a single long spray of orchids. If your flowers don't "reach" the stem, join them to the stem with short, light brush strokes. Bear in mind as you are creating this composition, that orchids will naturally bloom on alternating sides of the stem, so try to place blossoms on both sides and join them to the stem in an alternating pattern.

Chinese Orchid in Color

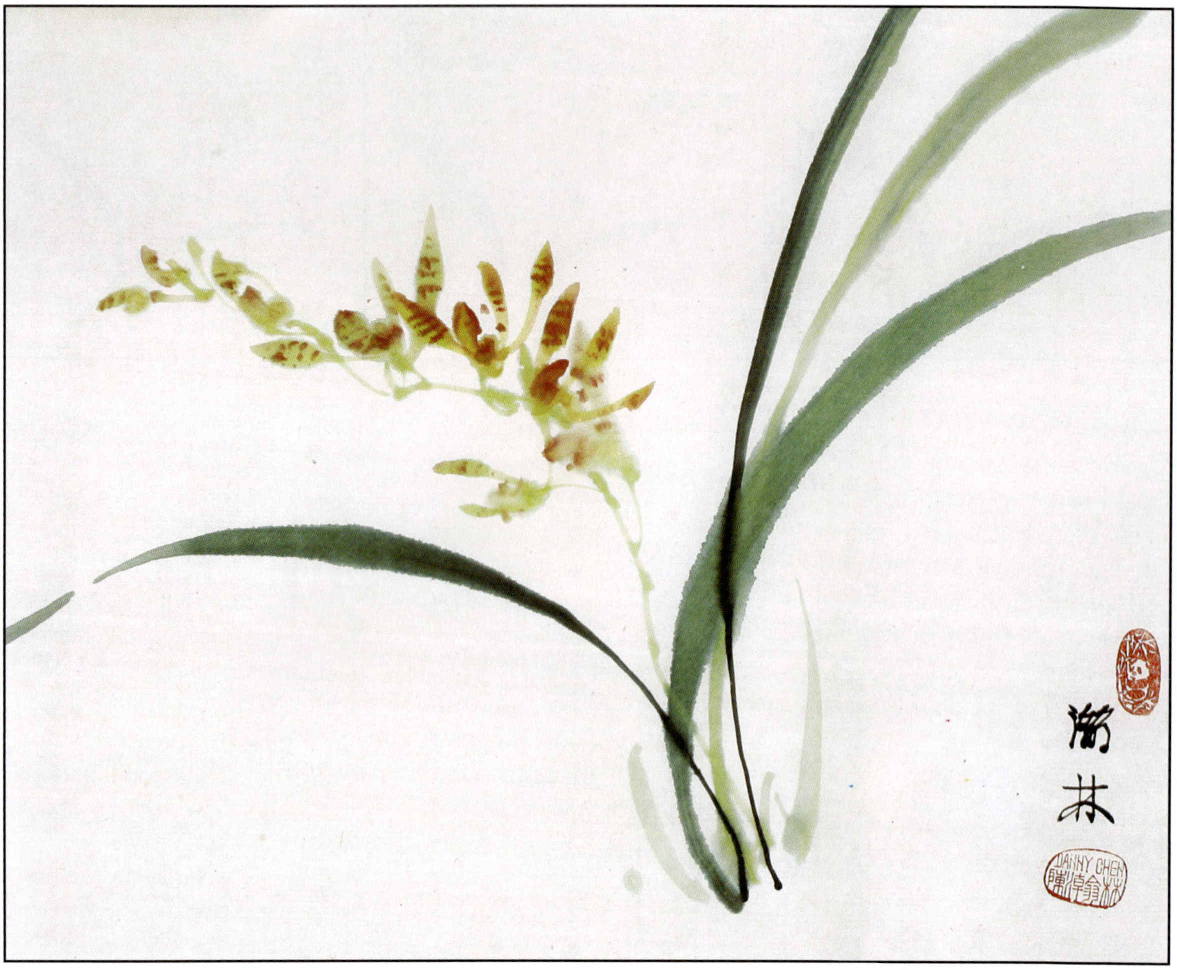

This is the same exercise as on the preceding pages, only now I will demonstrate the techniques that bring color to the page in Chinese brush painting. A distinguishing feature of the art form is how an artist can load a brush with multiple colors at one time to create variations, and manipulate how color releases from the brush onto the page. This allows for an endless range of color and tonal value. Herein the artist applies his mastery of control.

1.

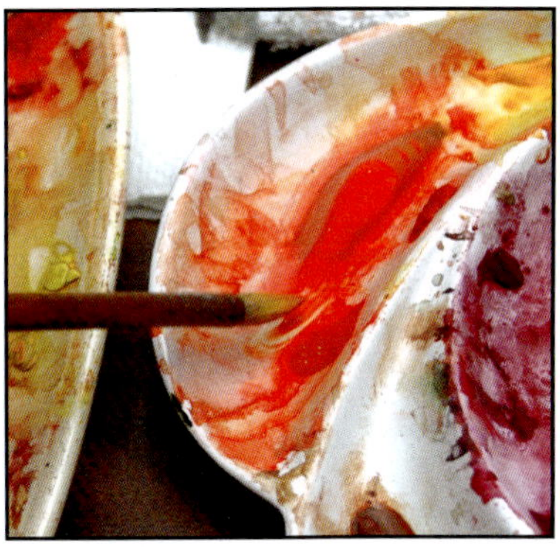

The first color you will mix is green, which you will mix from indigo and gamboge. To create a light green, use less indigo and more gamboge. To create a dark green, use more indigo and less gamboge. Mix your colors in a white ceramic dish or palette in order to clearly see your tones. Next put a small amount of gamboge and carmine in another dish. If you blend a small amount of carmine with water, you will achieve a lighter tone of red. If you blend a small amount of this lighter red with gamboge, you can create a mixed orange which I use in other demonstrations.

2.

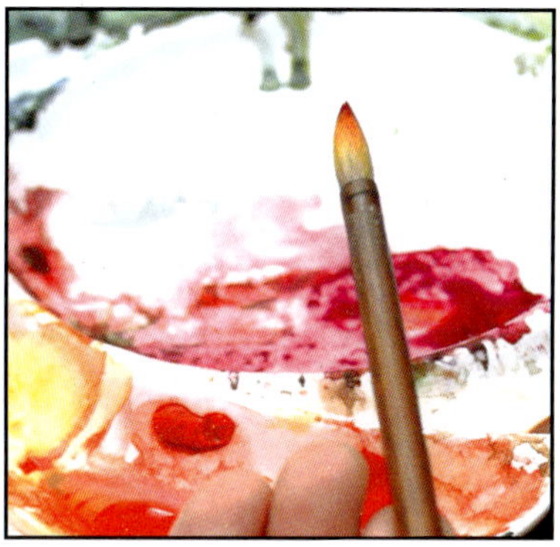

Load your whole brush completely with gamboge. Once you have the yellow on your brush, pick up carmine — halfway up your brush. Then, put a small amount of concentrated indigo just the tip of your brush.

3.

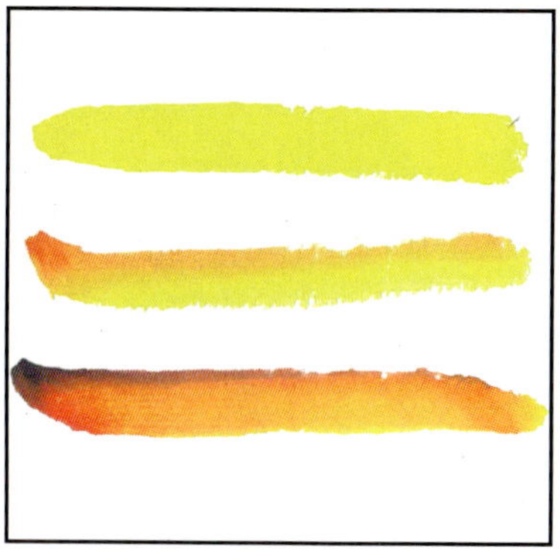

Practice making a number of strokes on sketch paper to see the results of loading color onto your brush in this manner. Try loading other colors in a similar fashion to see how the color tones change with each stroke. Try loading only two colors and see how these strokes appear as well. Finally, practice the same color loading and brush stokes with all three brushes to see the differences between each brush.

4.

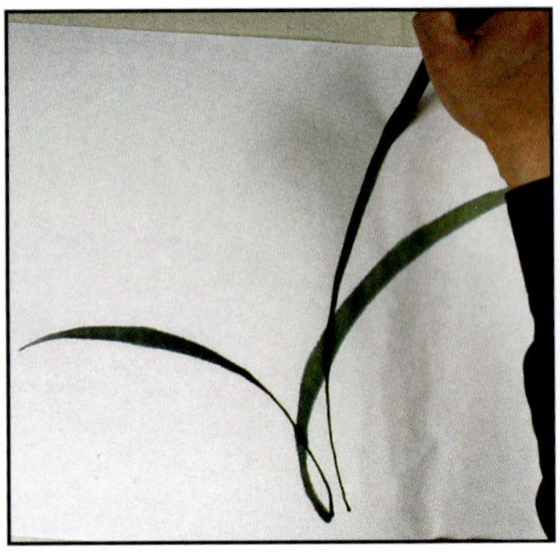

5.

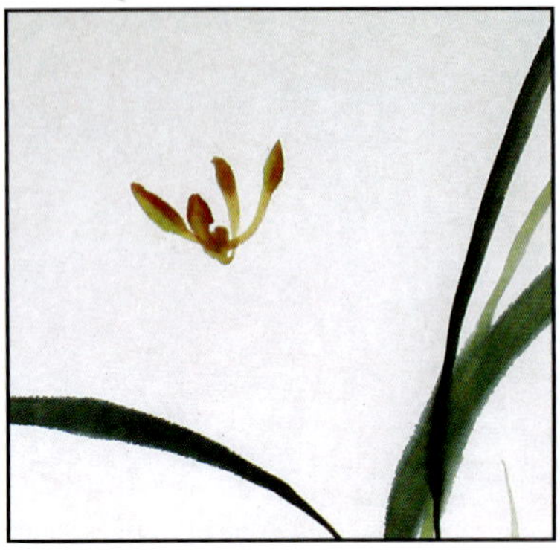

6.

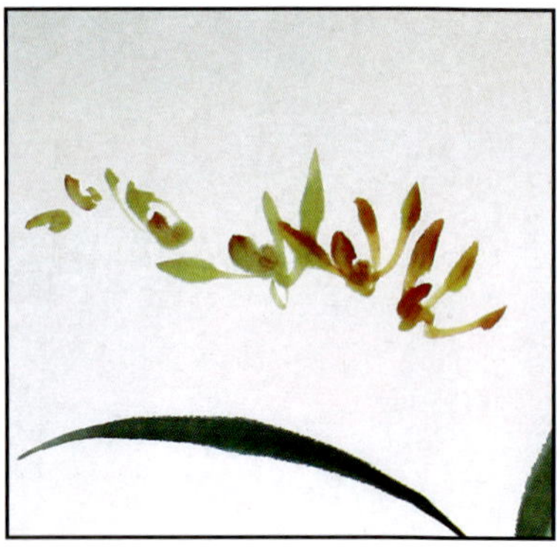

To paint the orchid in color, load your Orchid Bamboo brush fully with dark green paint, and then with black ink on the tip. Hold your brush with your hand positioned high on the handle to achieve a sense of flowing motion, and create the first leaf in the same manner you did in the previous demonstration. Reload ink onto the tip of your brush and using the same hand position, paint the second leaf, creating the "eyelet" at the bottom of the leaves. As you continue to add the leaves of the orchids, pay attention again to the tonal value of the paint and ink. If you continue to paint without reloading ink, the leaves are going to become progressively lighter, and recede in the composition. This technique brings depth and movement to the composition and is an important technique to become comfortable with.

Use your White Cloud brush, and load it fully with light green, then with medium carmine half way, and finally with concentrated carmine on the tip. Follow the same series of strokes that you used in the previous demonstration to create the little buds and flowers of the orchid. These strokes —14, 15 and 16, are demonstrated again on page 10. I start with the buds that are in full bloom, which would be on the "center" of the stem, and work down to the base of the stem. Use a diluted green for the blooms that are behind others on the stem.

Still using your White Cloud brush, loaded fully with light green, medium carmine and concentrated carmine on the tip, create the buds at the top of the stem, using only stroke14, without the larger petals.

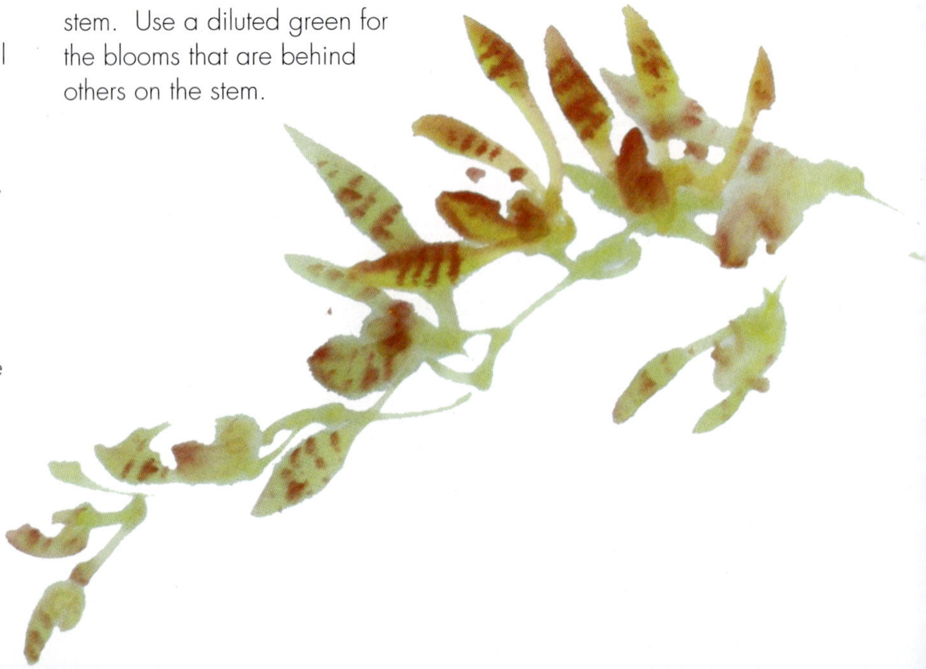

7.

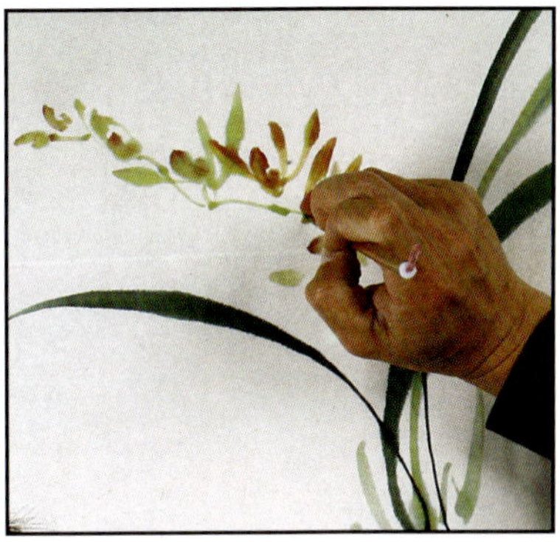

Use the Vine brush, load it fully with light green and concentrated carmine on one side only, half way. Flip your brush so that the carmine is on the top of the brush, and using stroke 7, create the stem of the orchid spray starting at the top bud. Join the buds to the stem in an alternating pattern as you did in the previous demonstration. By loading color on one side of the brush only, and then painting with the reverse side of the brush, the color on top bleeds to the outside edges of the bristles. This means that the predominant color you are painting with is the one you fully loaded onto the brush, but the second color works as an accent, creating a shadowed depth to the color in a single stroke. It is a lovely technique to use and is worth practicing until you can see the effect you are trying to achieve.

8.

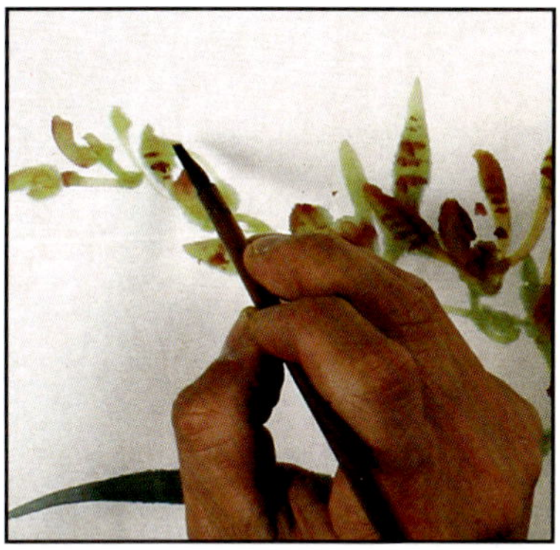

Use the Vine brush and pick up medium carmine and splay the bristles of the brush open by twisting them on the palette. Proceed to gently add bands of color to the petals of each flower using just a touch of the splayed bristles to the petals. Note that you will only add these bands of colors to the larger open petals, and not to the individual little buds.

9.

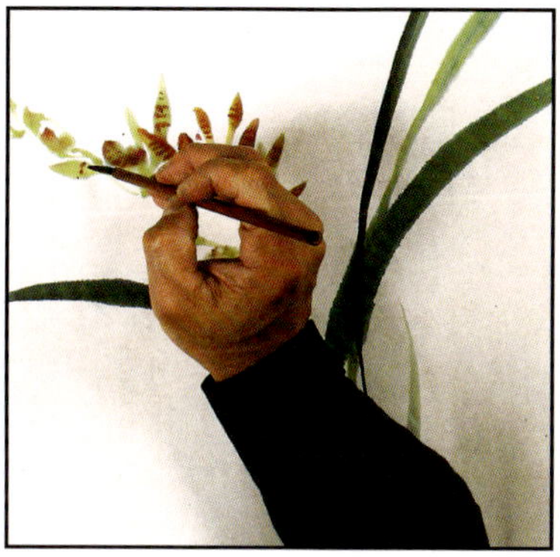

Add the stamen to the buds using the Vine brush with concentrated carmine. These are three little dots of color to the buds of the open blossoms. The banding on the orchids is not traditional to Chinese painting, as these types of orchids are not popular in China. However, because these orchids are common here in the west, I have developed this technique of adding color to the petals so that we can represent the flowers we see in our own world. In this way you as the artist can also develop your own personal style while learning to paint in the traditional manner.

Prawns

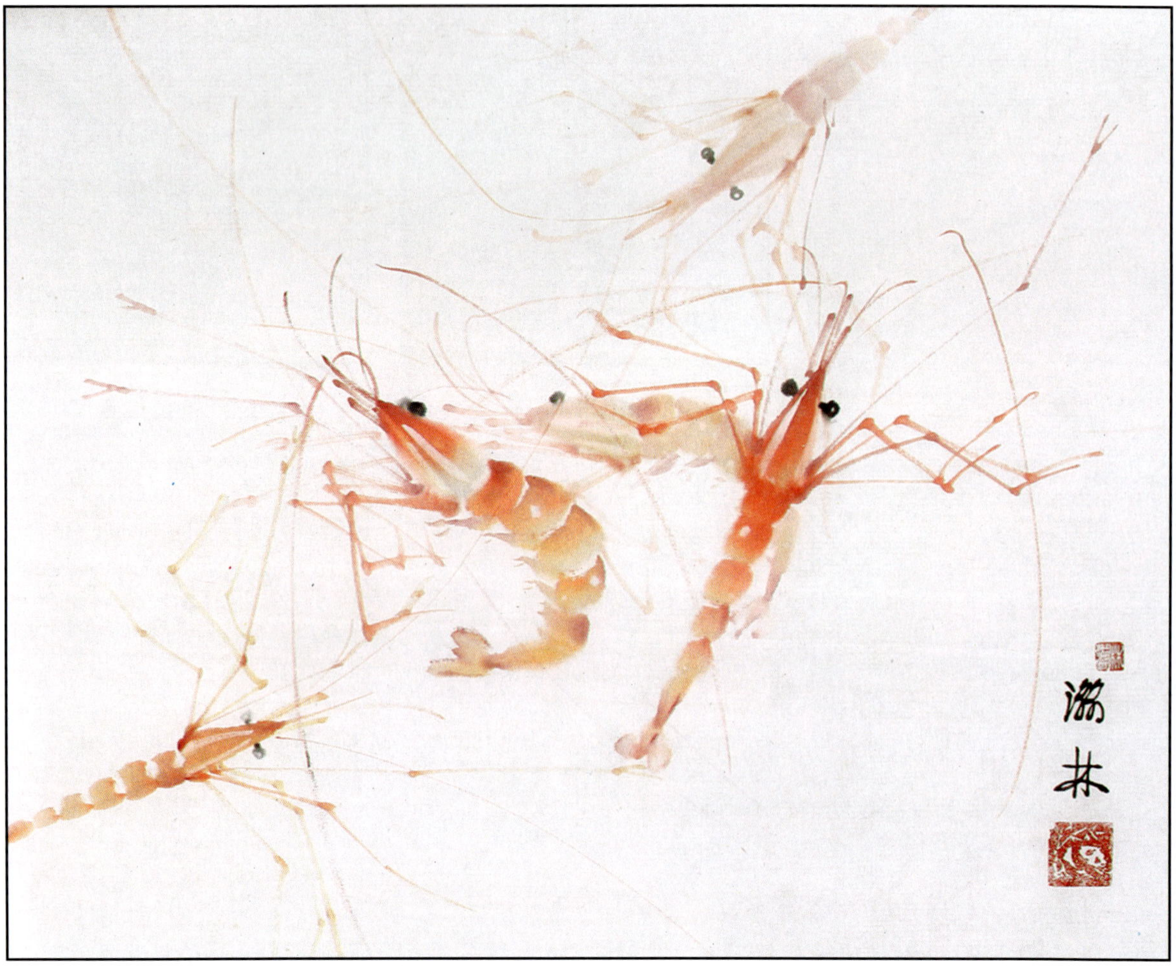

I love to do this exercise with students because it is easy to do and further exemplifies my belief that Chinese brush painting should not be so rigidly tied to tradition or that an individual artist should feel inhibited in painting subjects from the world around them. In the Pacific Northwest, the type of prawn that I paint here is common and bountiful, and produce fantastic paintings that is similar to the traditional Chinese subject of shrimp, but is more relevant to our own culture on this side of the ocean.

1.

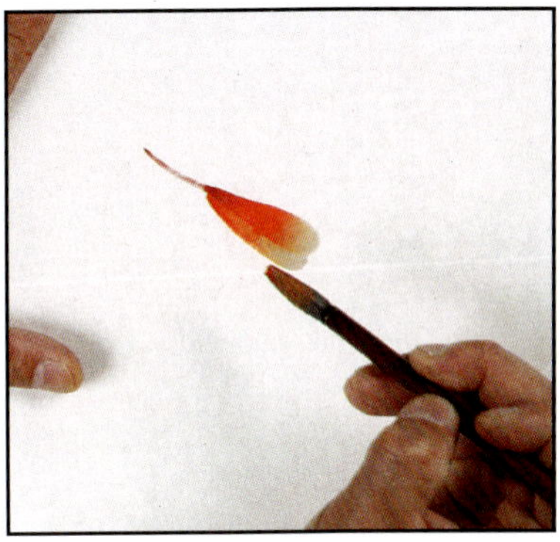

With a Vine brush, I combine gamboge and carmine to create a mixed orange color. Fully load the mixed orange onto the brush, with a bit of carmine on the tip. I am first going to create the spike on the head of the prawn with a simple downward stroke. Next, use the White Cloud brush and load it with mixed orange. Pick up carmine on the tip. You are going to create the head of the prawn in two strokes, the first being the "top" side of the head, and the second stroke the underside of the head, without reloading the brush. Start the first stroke at the base of the spike, with the tip of your brush touching it, and pull the stroke down to create the elongated head. Start the second stroke in the same spot, and lay the stroke down beside the first, just overlapping it.

2.

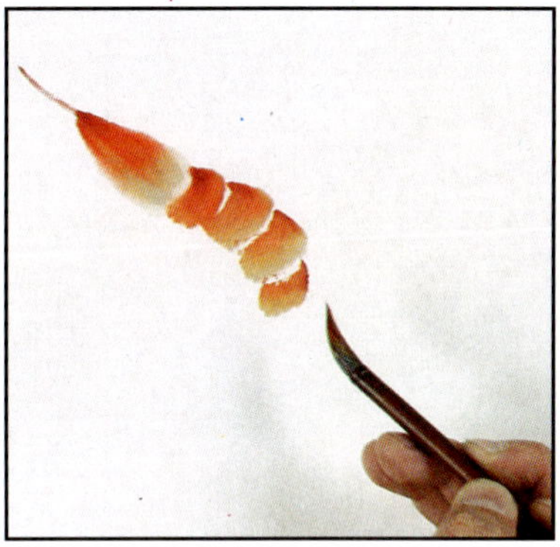

To create the body, load your brush in the same way that you did for the head. Now however, you are going to make a series of four progressively smaller side strokes to create each segment of the body. Tilt your brush to a 45 degree angle off the paper, and starting with the tip of your brush at the base of the head, you are going to "push" the stroke, from right (or the back of the prawn) to left (to the belly of the prawn) in a shallow stroke that curves around the base of the head. Again, you want to achieve the transition from dark to light to create dimensionality in the prawn.

3.

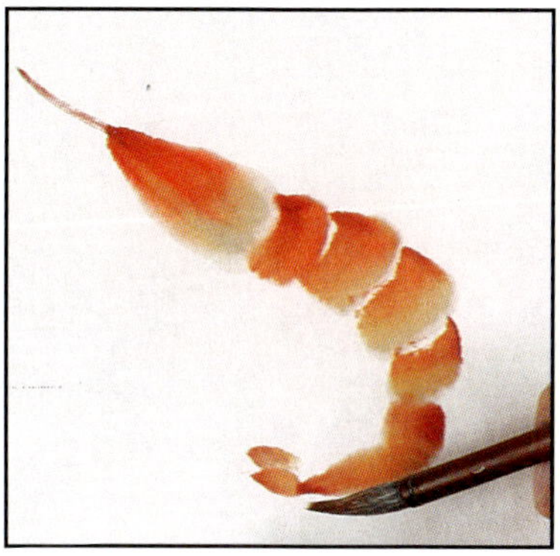

Reload your brush with the two colors to create the tail. Start at the end of the tail, and using a side stroke, drag or pull the stroke up to the last section of the prawn. Add a tiny short stroke for the tip of the tail. Finally, dip your brush tip in water to dilute the mixed orange on your brush, pick up a touch of carmine on the tip of your brush, and paint the two little wings on each side of the tip of the tail, pulling up towards the tip.

Brush Techniques

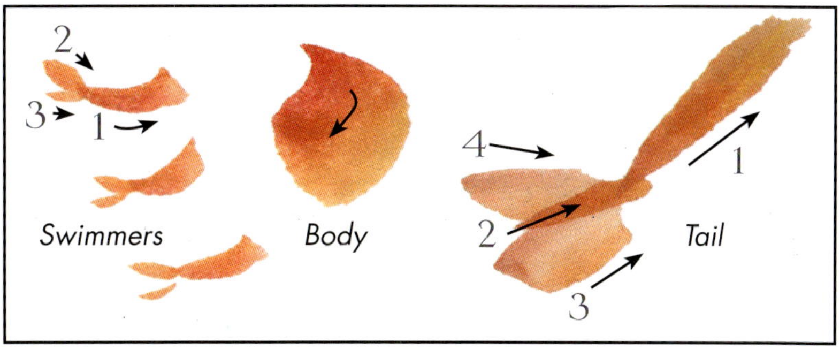

Here is a closer look at the coloring for the body sections as well as the strokes that make up the tail and swimmers.

4.

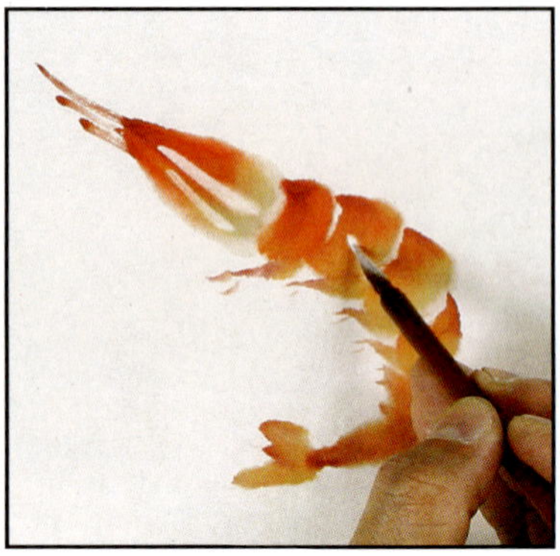

Reload the carmine and make quick, light strokes along the body sections of the prawn to make a series of little swimming legs. Add the highlights to the body by using concentrated white on your Vine brush. Pull two short strokes of white on the "underside" of the prawn head, and small highlight spots on the sections of body.

5.

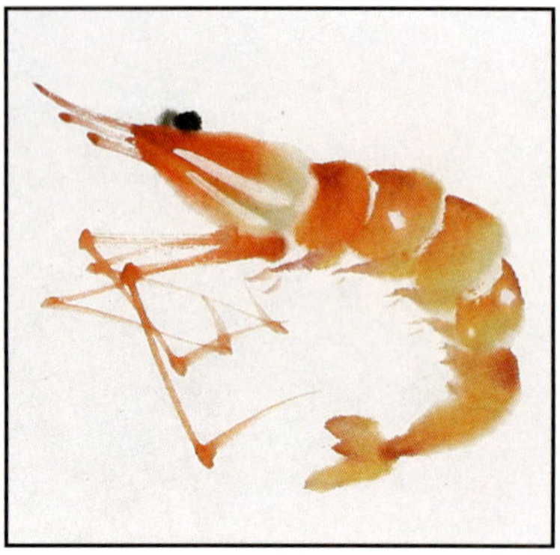

Add eyes by dotting on ink with your Vine brush —it should be quite dry or the ink will spread out and you will have huge eyes on your prawn. Try to picture the position of the eyes as though you were holding a prawn in your hand at the same angle. Would you see both eyes or just one? Would they be positioned forward on the head or further back? Add four legs to your prawn. Fully load mixed orange on your Vine brush and pick up concentrated carmine on the tip. Flip your brush so that the carmine is on the top. The legs are joined at the base of the head and are painted in three sections. Pull your strokes quickly and lightly, and almost "flick" your brush off the paper with the last stroke. Add two more long legs coming out the front that have two little claws attached.

6.

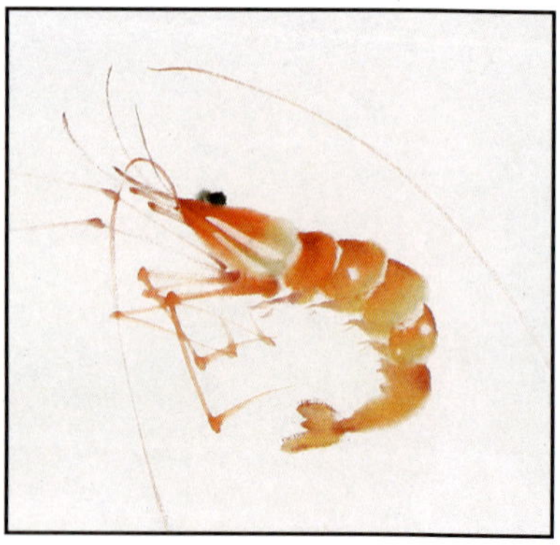

Prawns have ten legs, but you may not want to paint in all of them, depending again on the position of the prawn in your composition. It may appear jumbled and awkward, so I usually will paint four legs if my prawn is on its side, and add in more if I feel it necessary. When I am painting a prawn from a bird's eye perspective however, I will paint in the correct number of legs as it makes sense visually and logically that we would see all of the legs. As an artist, it is up to you to interpret nature how you feel best expresses what you wish to portray. To finish the prawn, I will add antennae and whiskers. I paint two long antennae with the Vine brush loaded with mixed orange and carmine. Each antenna is two strokes, the first starting at the top of the head directly forward, the second arcing out into whichever direction you wish the antenna to point. A prawn has four whiskers — two long ones and two short ones.

Brush Techniques

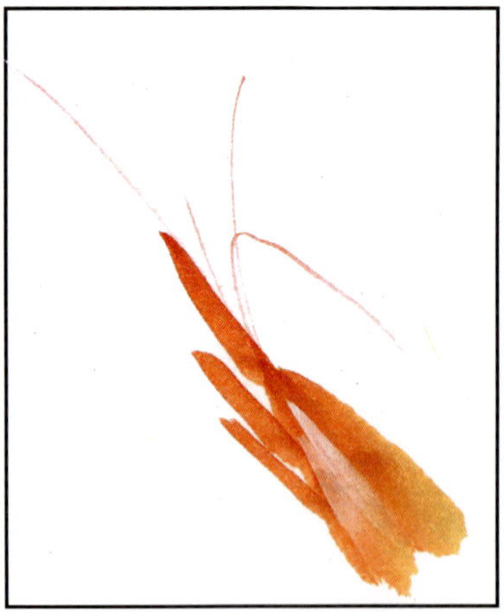

Here is a closer look at the swimmers, whiskers and antennae from the side.

7.

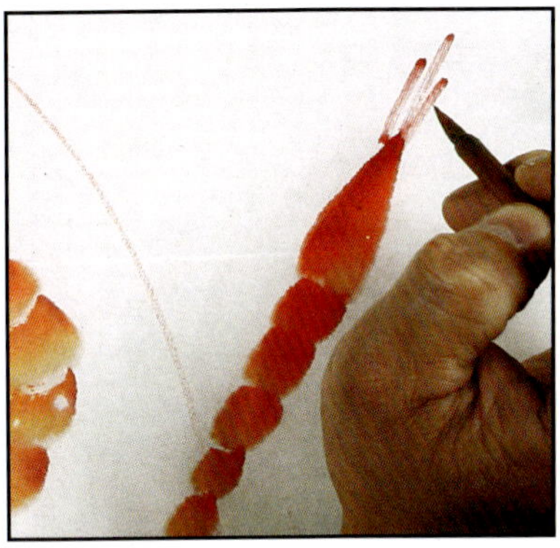

Repeat steps number 1, 2 and 3 to add a second prawn in your composition. We are looking at this prawn from the top, and we see the body elongated, rather than curved. From the top, we see all three of the "spikes" that are attached to the prawn's head. The middle one is the longest one, and the remaining two are shorter and to each side. Also paint the sections of the body in a straighter line, rather than curved, but using the same side stroke as you did for the first prawn. Notice now that you don't see the swimmers on the prawn as they are on the underside of the body.

8.

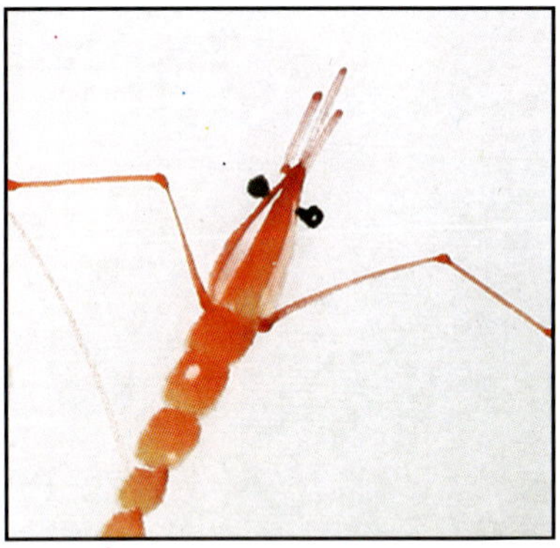

Add in the eyes and highlights as you did on the first prawn. Then start to add in the legs. Notice in this image how the legs are now evenly paired on each side of the body, and I will add in a total of ten including the claws- five on each side. The stroke is the same, but the direction is different, starting at the base of the head and working directly away from the body in three strokes. The pair of claws also start at the base of the head, and are painted almost pointing directly out the front head.

9.

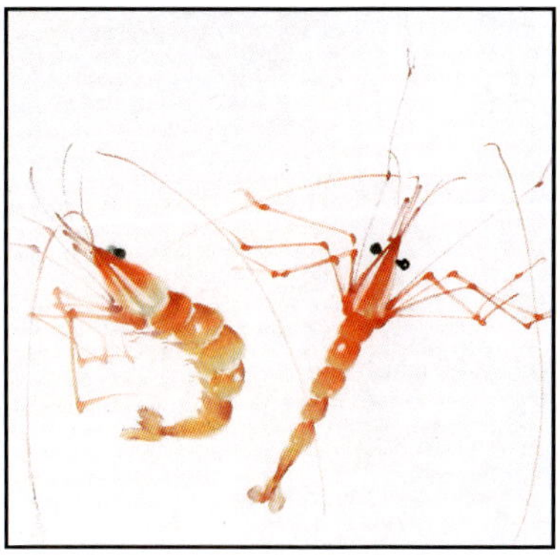

Finish the prawn by adding the antennae and whiskers much the same way as you did for the first prawn. Again, the whiskers are painting in two pairs — one long and one short. You may want to continue adding more prawns to your composition in different positions, from different angles, and in different tones; lighter prawns behind and darker prawns in front.

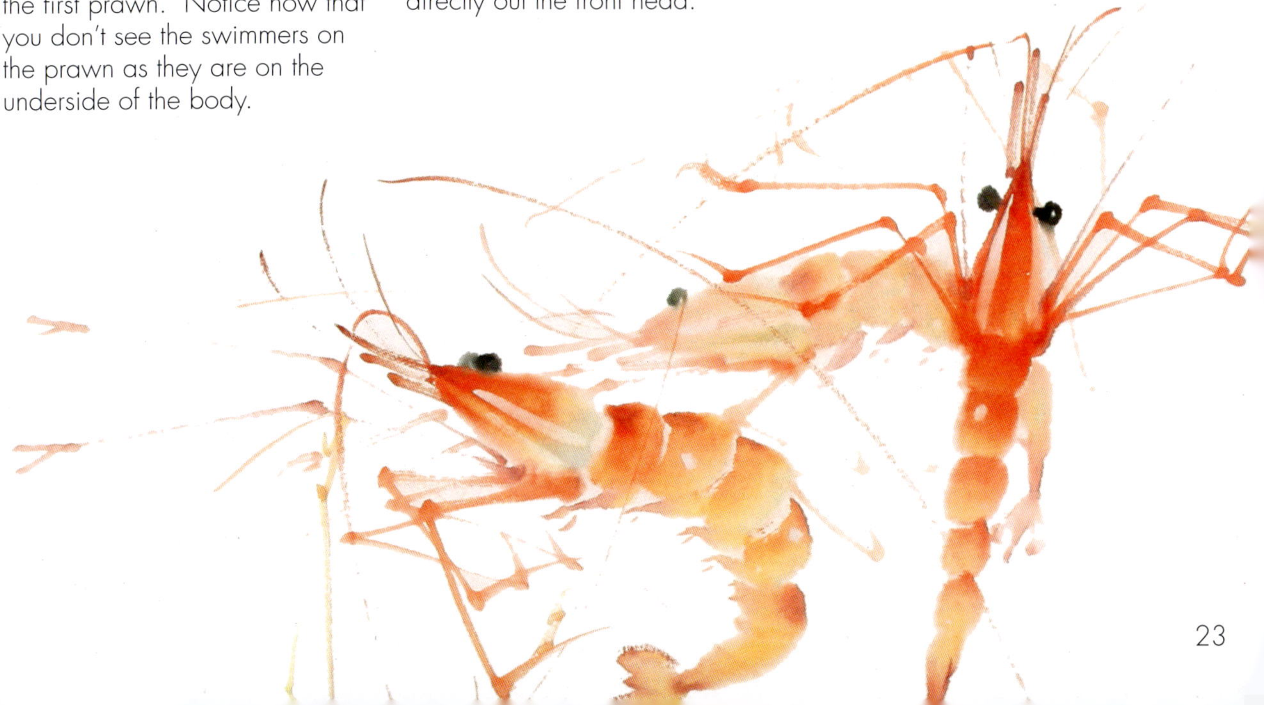

Baby Chicks

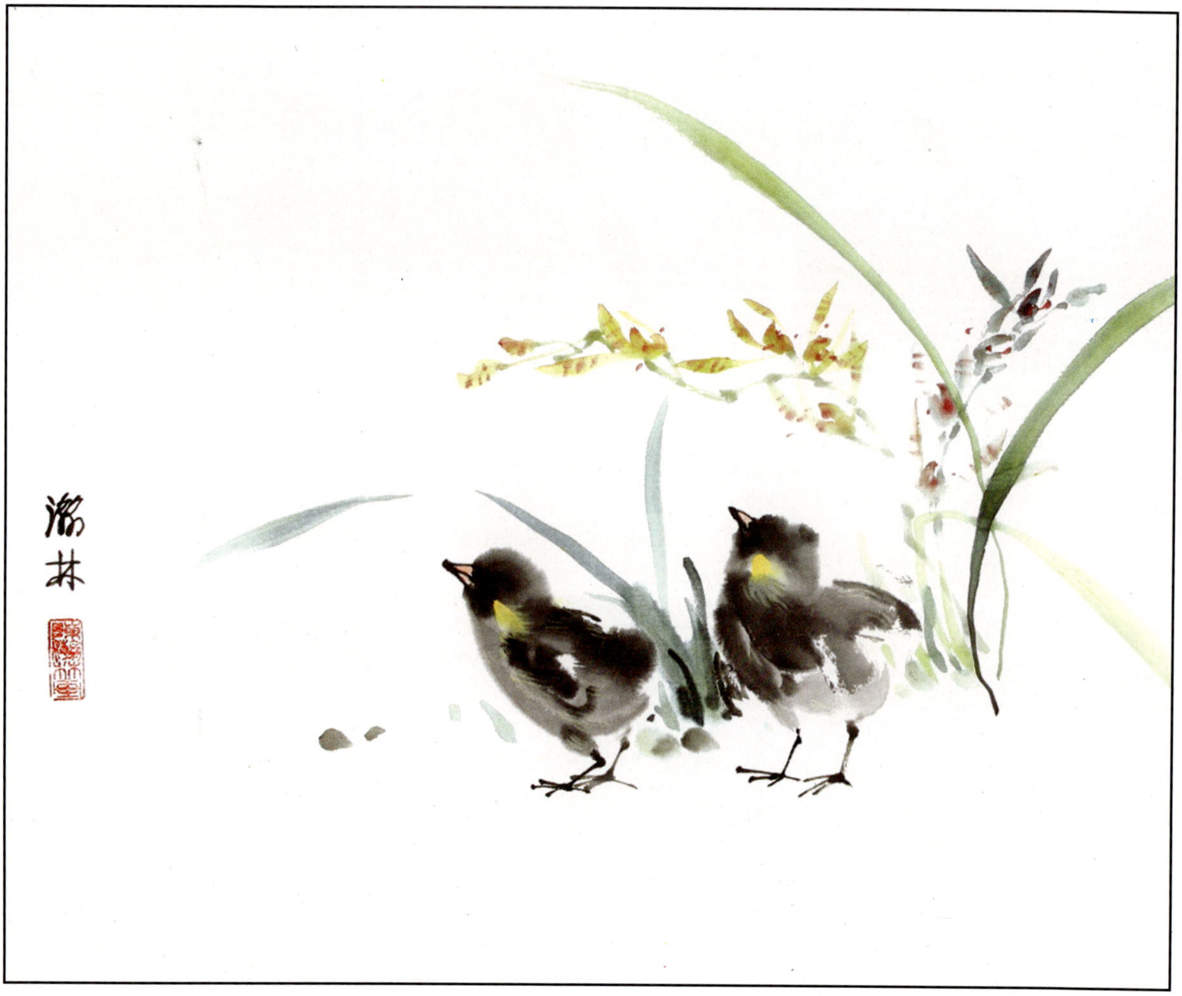

This demonstration emphasizes skills for learning to load your brush with ink to create different tones, as well as to paint using the side of the brush to achieve maximum paint coverage. The strokes needed to create these chicks are 18 through 21 on page 10, and they are worth practicing before you start the demonstration. This demonstration also shows how the properties of xuan paper can be used to help achieve the "fluffy" effect for the baby chicks, painted in two different profiles.

1.

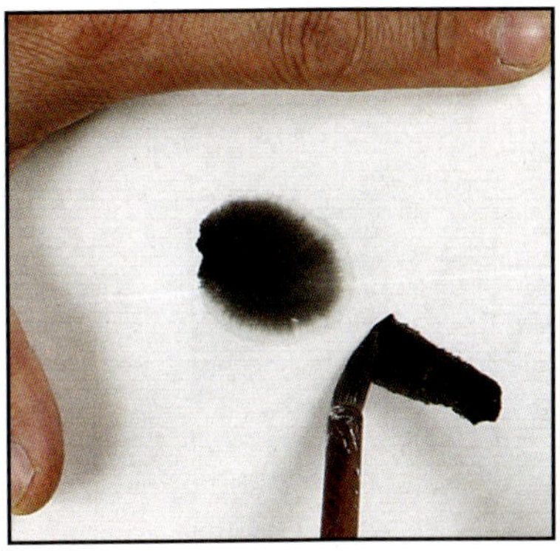

I begin with my White Cloud brush, which I load with medium ink and the tip with concentrated ink. I will make stroke 18, whereby I lay the bristles fully onto the paper and make a small pushing stroke angling upwards to paint the oval head of the chick.

2.

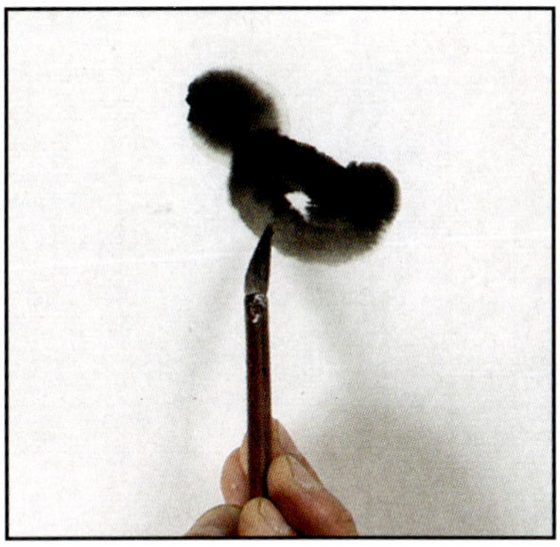

The body is made with two strokes. Push the first oval stroke from the tail around the top of the body and all the way around back again to the tail using a side stroke in a counter clockwise direction. You will touch the tip of your bristles to the base of the head as you create this oval stroke. The second stroke is a small sidestroke for the chick's tail. If there is a small area that is not filled in the center by the stroke, do no worry as you can use this spot in the pattern of feathers.

3.

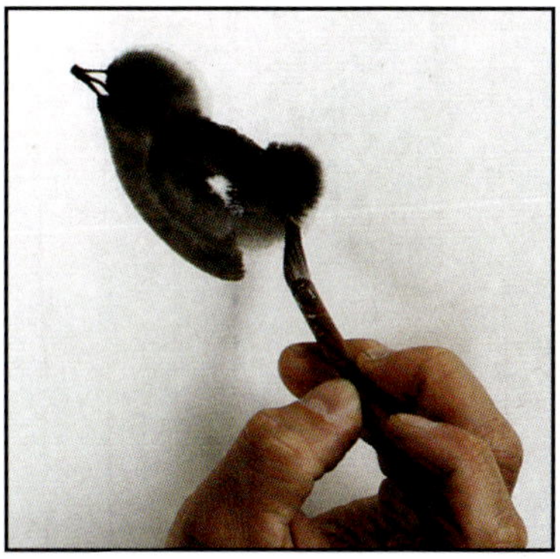

Next, use your Vine brush and load concentrated ink onto it to add the chick's beak. Then you are going to complete the chick's body with three more strokes using your White Cloud brush loaded with light ink and the tip with concentrated ink. The first stroke is the chick's throat, starting from beneath the beak, pressing down at the start and lifting at the chest. Press down immediately again to create the second stroke and drag towards the base of his tummy in a straight line. Finish the third stroke by changing direction and starting from back of the chick under its tail and joining the stroke that was just completed.

Here are the strokes for the throat and tummy.

Brush Techniques

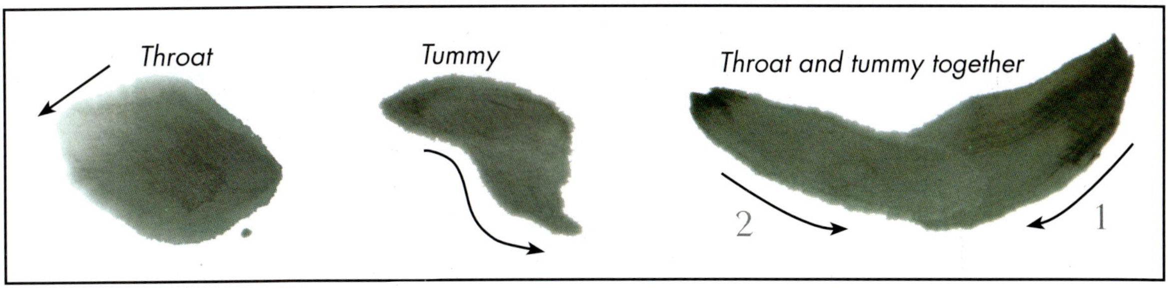

4.

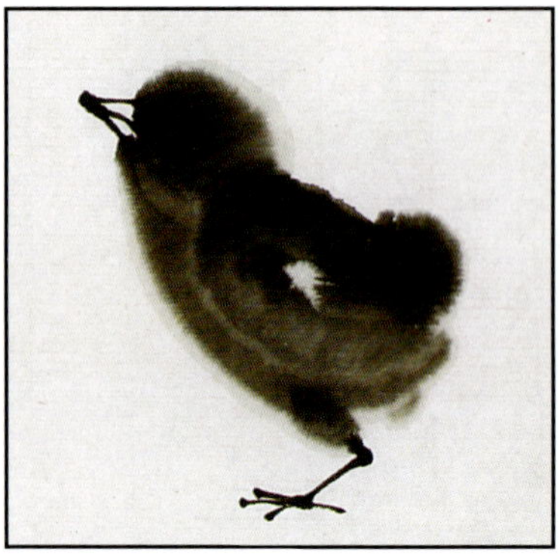

Use your White Cloud brush for the chick's drumstick at the join of your last two strokes. Load the tip of the brush with a medium tone of ink and press down to create a small mark, without pulling the stroke. Use the Vine brush to create the leg in six strokes (refer to stroke 21 on page 10). The first stroke starts at the top part of the leg from the drumstick, the second stroke completes the leg, the third, fourth and fifth strokes add the feet and a final short stroke adds the back claw. Make the second leg in the same manner without reloading your brushes with ink.

5.

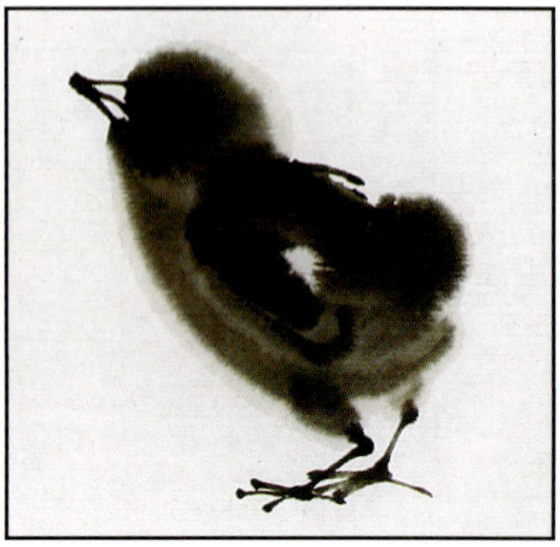

To give your chick's wings shape, you are going to add three "hook" strokes to the body of the chick where you want the wings to lay. Again, remember that wings move in many different ways and directions. There isn't one "ideal" stroke for this step, rather place the strokes in as you see appropriate for your baby chick.

6.

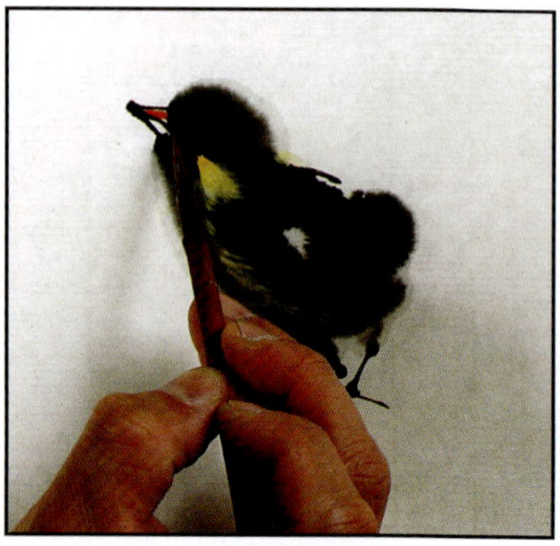

With the White Cloud brush, load white and pick up gamboge on the tip to press a small mark into the neck of the chick to create the bright feathers. Then, on a piece of scrap paper or in your dish, wipe off the excess paint, and splay the bristles of the brush out, to create a fan-like shape. Use your brush in this way, with the bristles splayed to gently brush over the yellow patch of feathers, as well as the wings to create a soft, feathery texture.

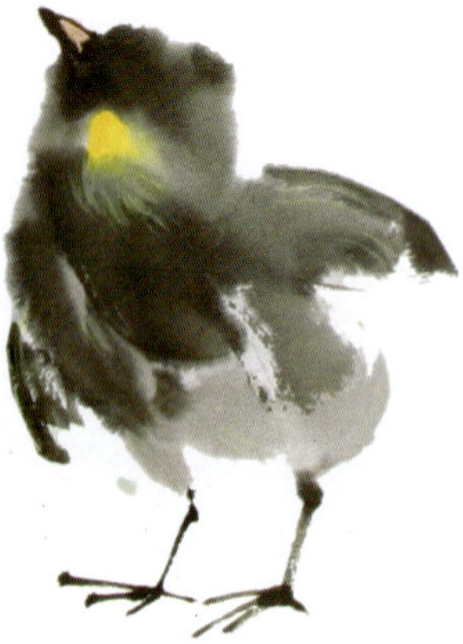

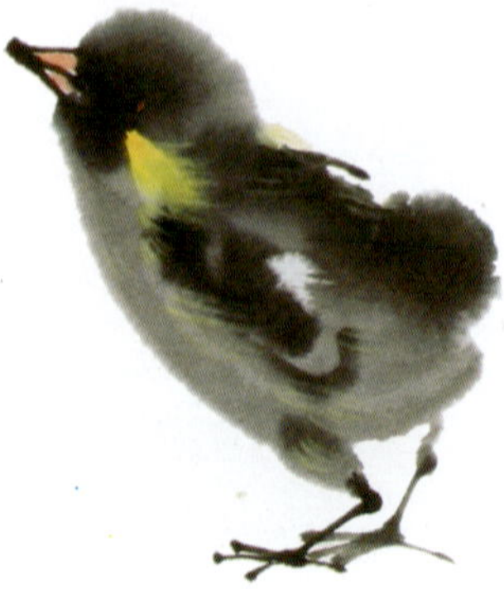

7.

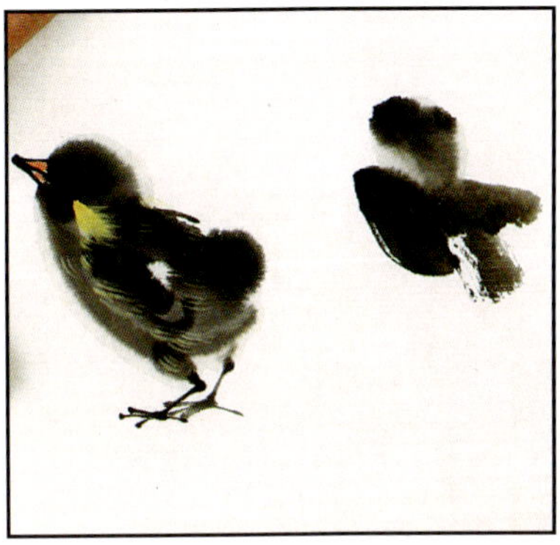

Now add a second chick to your scene in a different pose, with his wings open slightly. I start in the same way as I made the first. I place the head slightly higher on the body as he is stretching up with his neck. I am using a lighter tone of black so that this chick will have different coloring than the first chick. Using medium ink on my White Cloud brush with concentrated ink on the tip, I am going to make the body of this chick using a stroke that I created to accomplish this in one stroke. In essence you are creating a squashed "w" shape with little hooks. Practice this stroke a few times on the scrap paper.

8.

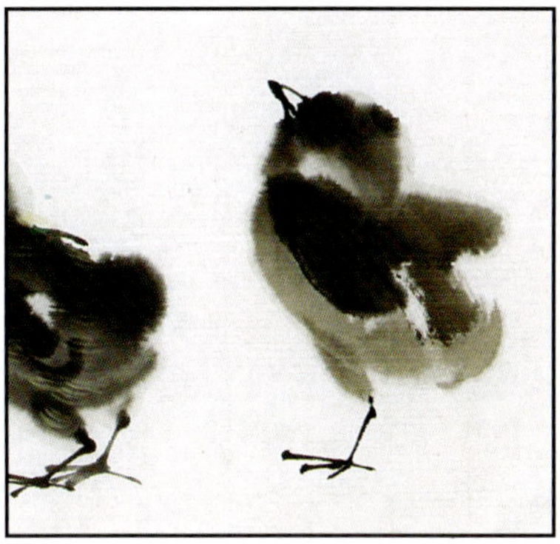

Add the beak with your Vine brush as you did in step 2. Use your White Cloud brush to finish the body with the same series of three strokes that you made in step 3 for the throat and tummy. Finally, add in the legs, starting with the drumstick and a light ink tone and your White Cloud brush. Finish with your Vine brush loaded with concentrated ink. Notice that this chick's feet are spaced differently than the first chick.

9.

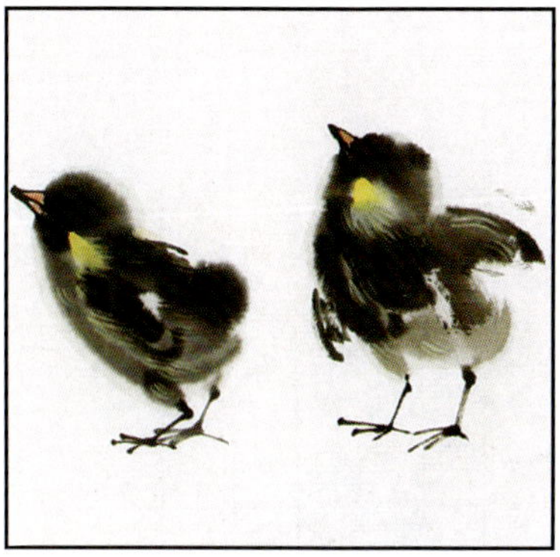

This chick's wings are open and flapping just a bit. Be free to express how much you wish them to be open or show movement by filling in more feathers using your Vine brush with concentrated ink. You may also want to add in the small piece of wing on the opposite side of the body-whatever you think you can see from the way your chick is standing. Finish off your chick by adding a patch of yellow feathers using the same technique you did for your first chick. In my final painting, I added the same orchid we used in our previous demonstration. Feel free to add your own orchids and grass to finish your composition.

Here are the strokes in step 5 and 7.

Brush Techniques

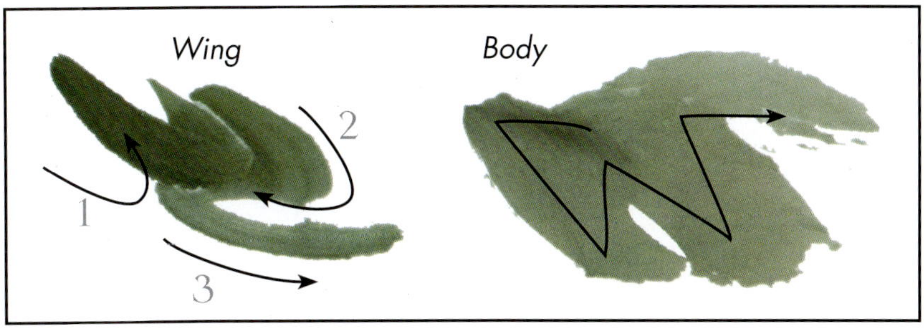

CRABS

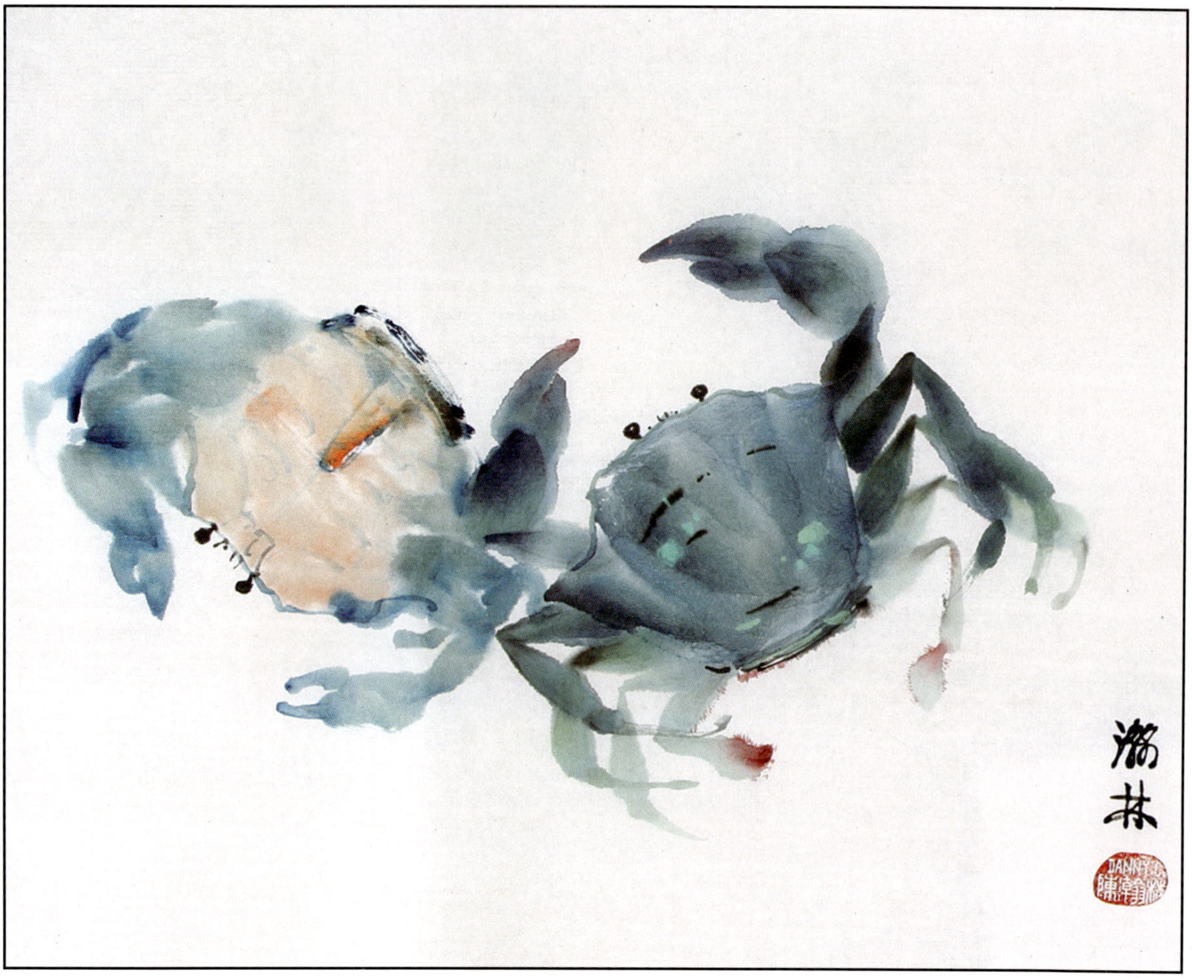

Here is another example of how I have found an alternate method to painting a traditional Chinese subject. While a crab is a quite a common subject in Chinese painting, it is almost always done in ink. I enjoy the sùbject, but wanted to bring my own interpretation. I felt that by adding color, I can better represent the crab found on our cold and rocky seashores. To make this blue tone, I have first mixed indigo and gamboge to create a dark green, and I paint with this green, as well as indigo. I use a touch of carmine to give the crab more life.

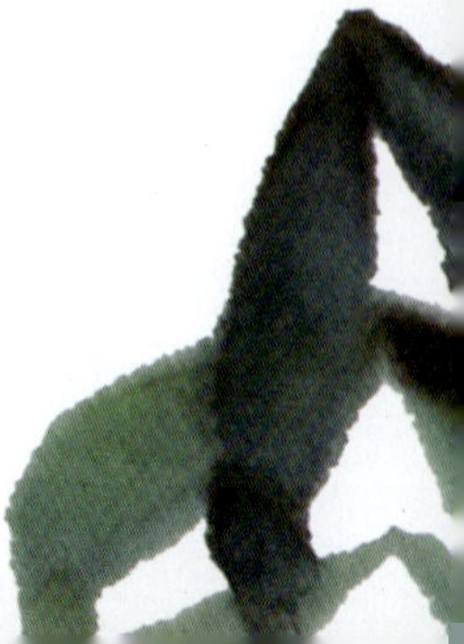

1.

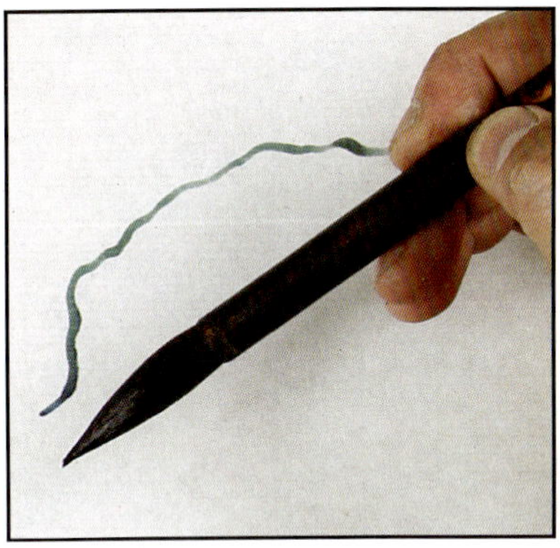

I begin by loading my Vine brush with dark green and outline the top half of body of the first crab. The intention is not to create an outline that is then painted in; merely to create a guide for the brush strokes that will make up the body of the crab. Use this line to guide the starting points for the next brush strokes you will make. You may want to practice sketching it on your pad a few times until you feel comfortable with this shape.

2.

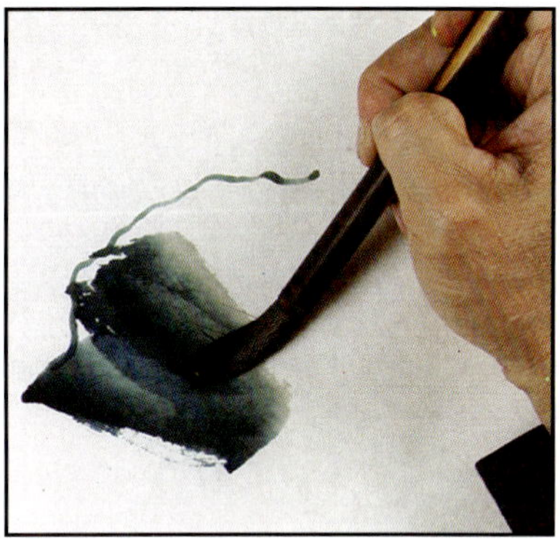

Using my Orchid Bamboo brush, load it completely with dark green, and the tip with indigo. Start the first stroke is by placing the bristles against the outside edge of the line you painted. I pull the stroke in and down, as you see indicated by the arrow on the next page. This creates the horn-like shape on the side of the shell. The second and third strokes are made without reloading the brush, and by pulling the strokes straight down; starting at the edge of your outline and lifting at the base of the shell. If you start a bit short of the edge of your outline don't be concerned, just try not to paint beyond it.

3.

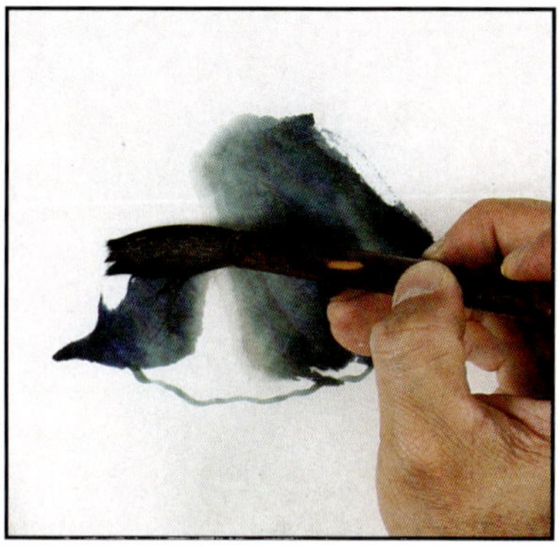

To finish painting in the shell, you may find it easier to rotate your paper roughly 90 degrees in a counter-clockwise position so that you don't have to turn your arm at an awkward angle to paint these next strokes. Reload your brush with dark green and indigo, and start the right side of the shell in the same manner; with your stroke starting at the edge of the outline, and pulling in and now up. Without changing the direction of your bristles or reloading your brush, make a second and third stroke by pulling the stroke up the back of the shell. In the end, you want the outer edges of the shell to be the darkest, and gradually lightening as you reach the center of the shell.

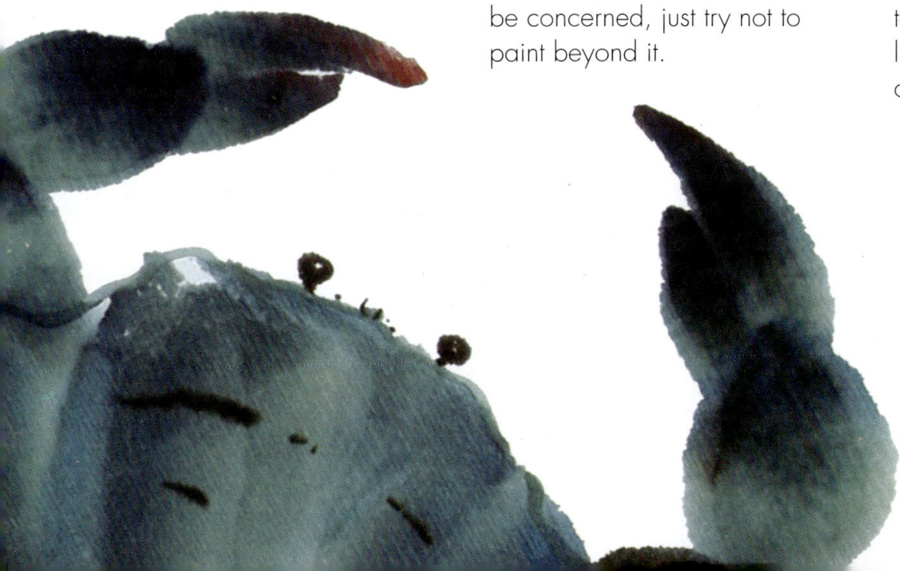

4.

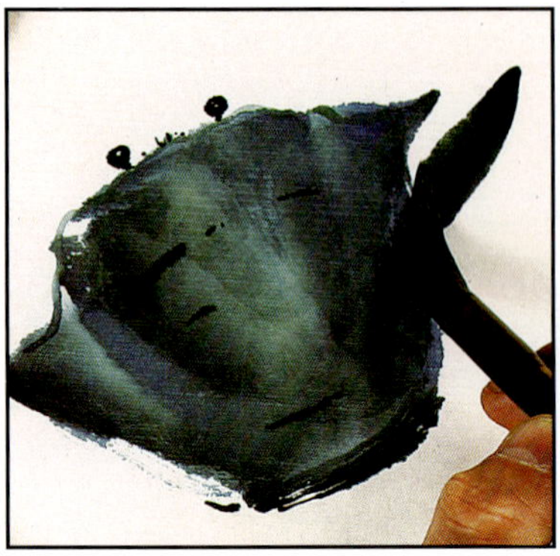

I add a few markings with my Vine brush and indigo ink onto the back of the crab, as well as a short quick stroke along the base of the shell to give it shape. I also add the eyes with my Vine brush and ink as well as short little antennae. I start to paint the legs for the crab using the Orchid Bamboo brush fully loaded with dark green, and pick up indigo at the tip. I paint the legs in three separate stokes, starting the first one away from the body and pulling in to the edge of the body to create the first joint.

5.

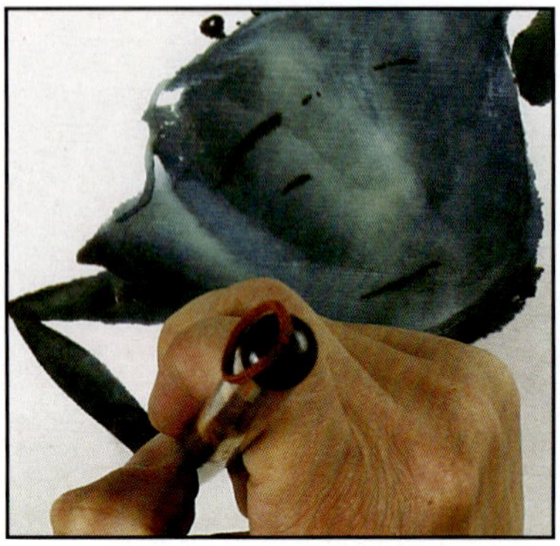

The second stroke of the leg will start at the tip of the first joint, and pull down to create the long center joint that widens at the end. Create the third joint by pulling a short, quick stroke off the second joint. This final stroke is a wide "nail heads rat's tail", stroke 7, with the base of the stroke wide, and tapering off as you pull it through. Reload your brush with the same dark green and indigo at the tip. Add the second leg of the pair on the opposite side using the same strokes.

6.

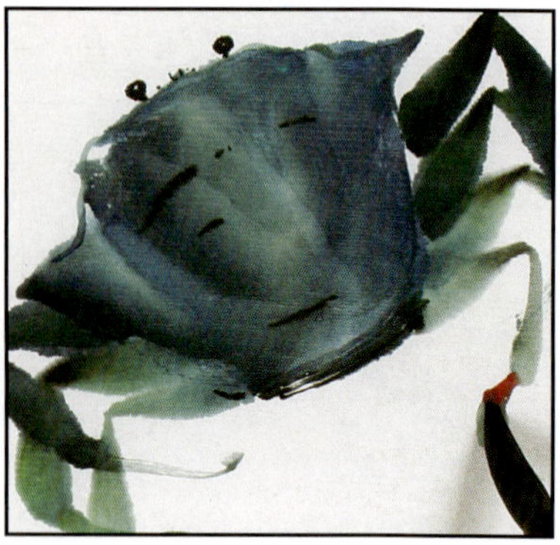

Continue to add the remaining three pairs legs down the side of the body using the same strokes as you did for the first. However, with each pair of legs, you will reload with a progressively lighter tone of green, and indigo at the tip. I add a dash of carmine to the tip of the last pair of legs.

Brush Techniques

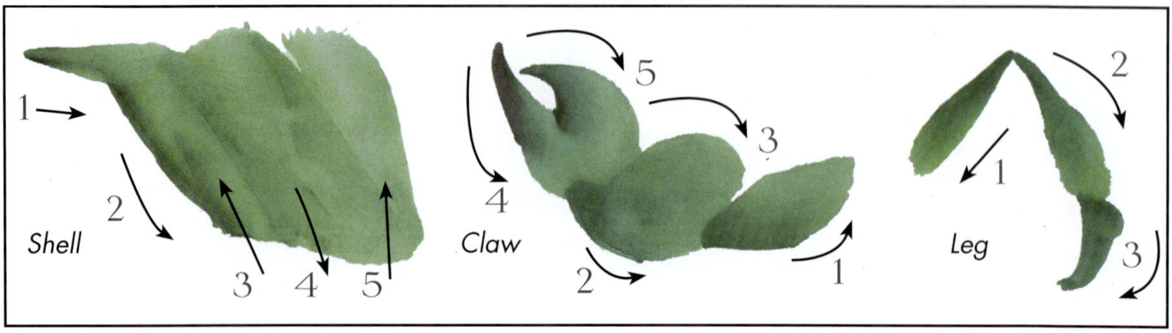

7.

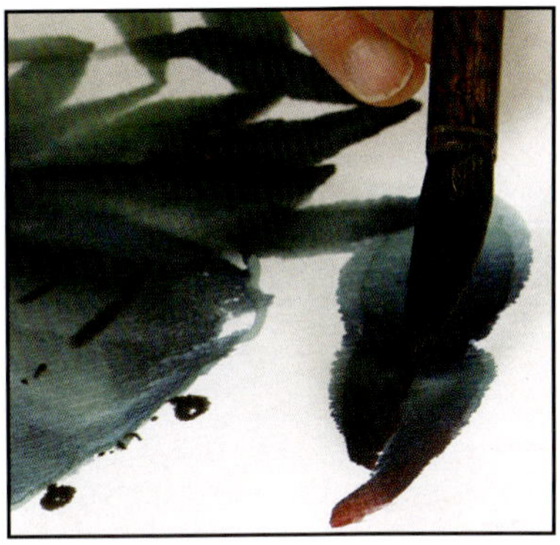

Now I start to work on the claws, by loading the Orchid Bamboo brush fully with dark green, and adding indigo to the tip. The first stroke is placed just above the first leg, starting out from the body and pulling into the shell. The claw is now made with a series of four strokes. Strokes one and two make the base of the claw, and strokes three and four make up the pincers. Load carmine on the tip of your brush on the third stroke. Add the second claw to the other side of the body in the same way.

8.

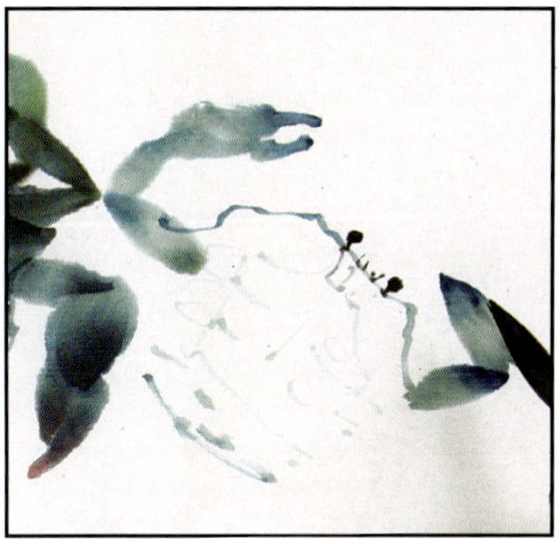

To begin the second crab I do an outline again, taking into consideration the position of the first crab. Because this crab is on its back the shape is a little rounder. Use your Vine brush as before, loaded with a medium green, and create more of the outline to give the crab shape. I continue with my Vine brush instead of using my Orchid Bamboo brush because I want to be able to show more detail of the underside of the crab. Once you finish the outline, load the Orchid Bamboo brush with a diluted, medium green with indigo at the tip and work out the legs and claws as you did before to create a softer, less defined crab.

9.

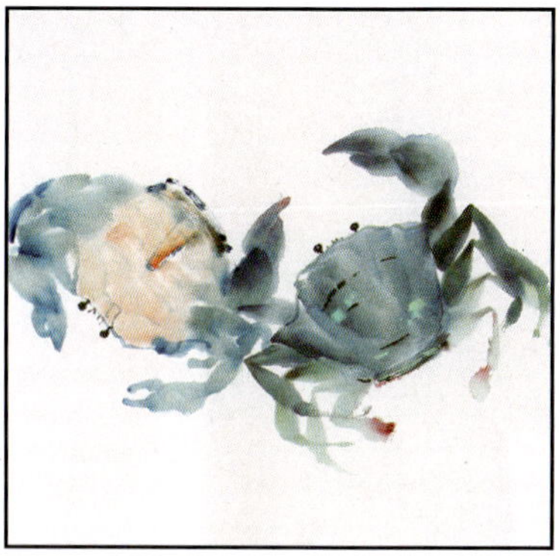

Finally, to mix the color for the belly of the crab, use carmine and gamboge to create a mixed orange, and then dilute the mixed orange before fully loading your brush. Fill in the underside of the crab with this color. Try varying the tone of this mixed orange to create interest and depth to this area of the crab. Add eyes, antennae and other final touches with your Vine brush to complete the second crab. You will see in the final image on page 28, that once I'm done I add my signature. With this composition I'll use the far right corner. In Chinese painting it is considered *feng shui*, or good luck, to never place anything in front of a living subject so as to not block the flow of "breath".

Birds of Paradise

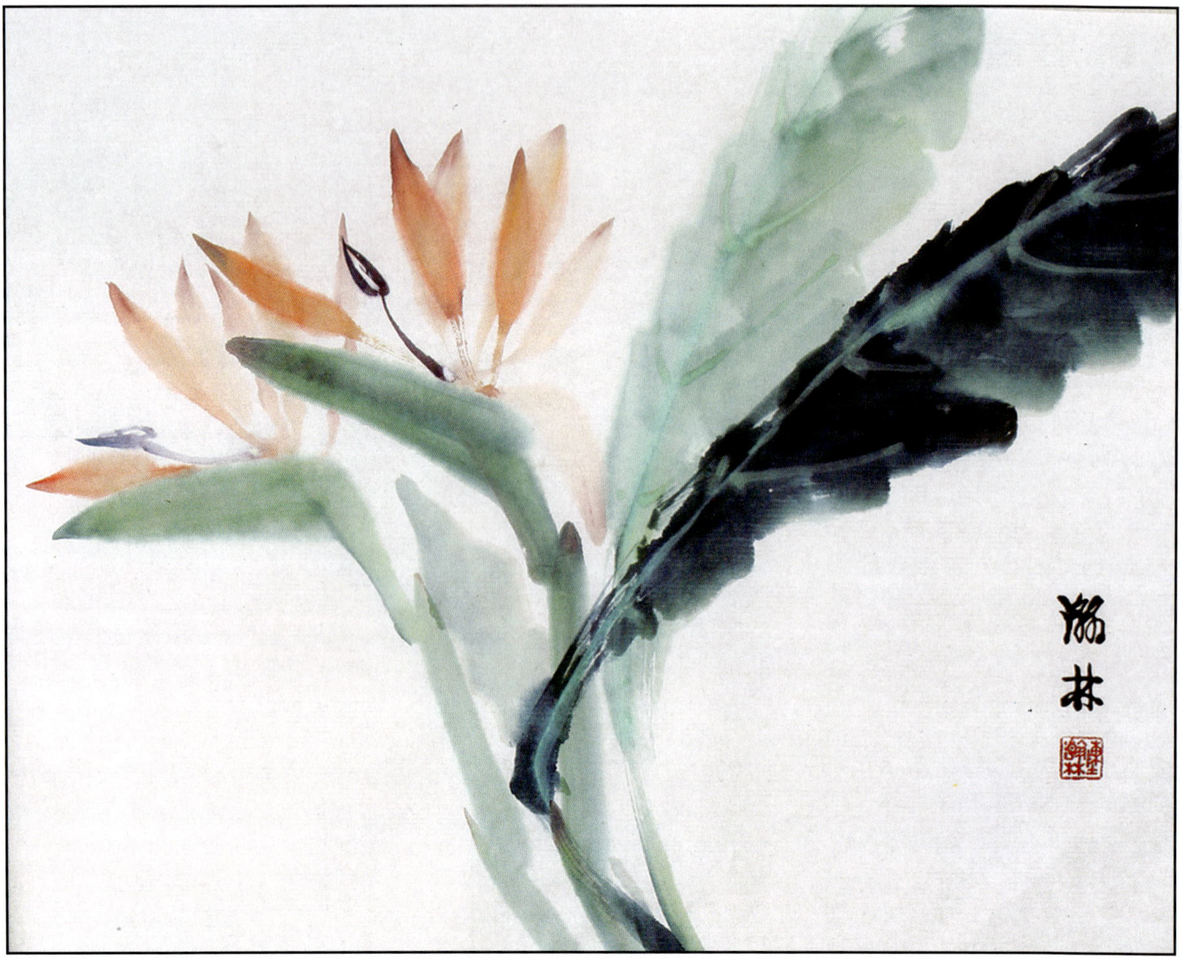

Birds of Paradise are a marvelous combination of a distinctive shape and brilliant colors. They bear beautiful, orange flowers with a deep purple stamen on a single thick stalk. The leaves are full and broad and are easy to paint. This is the first demonstration in which I use white to create an opaque color for the veins in the leaves and it is a good technique to know in order to create a color that you can use for detail work.

1.

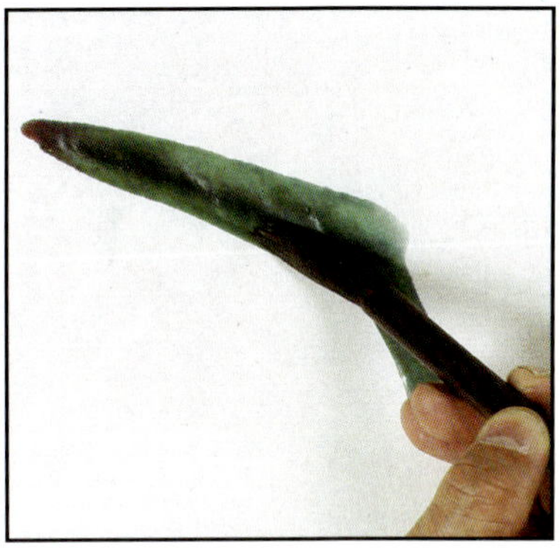

I begin with the stem using a mixture of dark green fully loaded on my Orchid Bamboo brush with carmine on the tip and stroke 17 on page 10. The top half of the stem is made in three strokes. The first from the tip of the stem along the top, the second stroke also starts at the tip of the stem, below the first stroke, pressing down along the stroke. As you get to the end of the second stroke, ease off on the pressure, and without lifting the brush off the paper, make the third stroke down the top section of the stalk.

2.

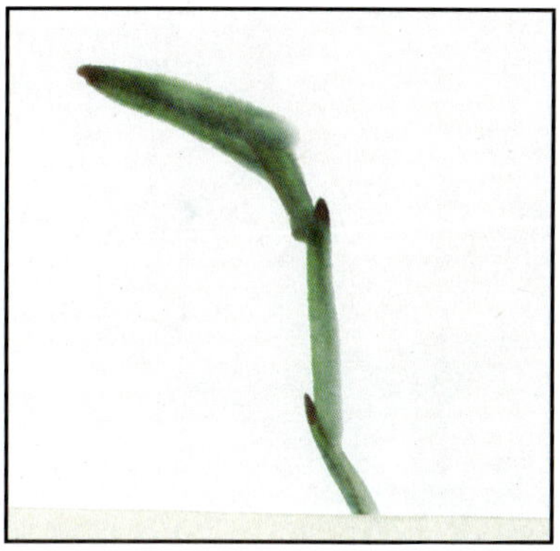

Reload your bush with medium green and carmine, and add two strokes to complete the stalk, alternating sides as you start each stroke.

3.

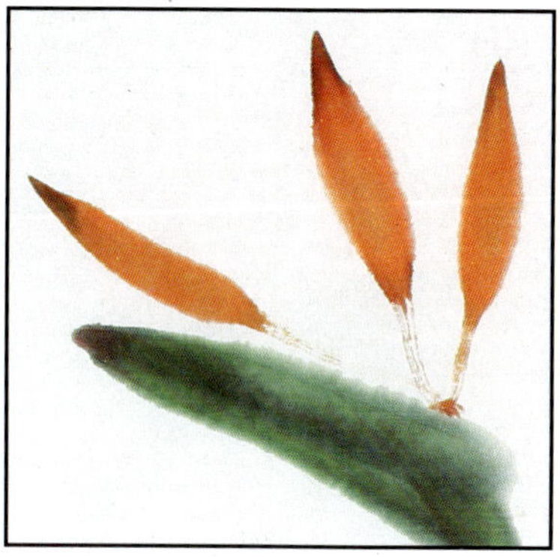

To create the flowers, use carmine and gamboge to create a mixed orange. Load it onto your brush, then load medium carmine on one side, and finally concentrated carmine on the tip. Flip your brush and using stroke 15, place the first petal about a third of the way in from the tip of the stem, tucking the base of the petal into stem. Reload the brush and add the second and third petals.

Here are up close images of a petal and stamen. Notice the beautiful colors that can be acheived by correctly loading your brush. Try to focus on improving your technique in this demonstration.

Brush Techniques

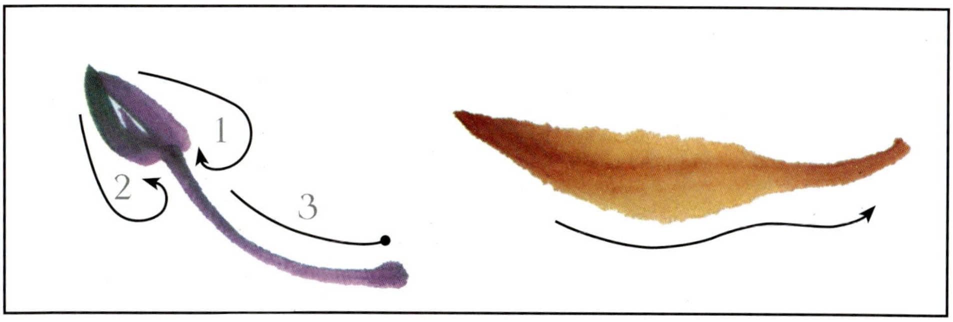

4.

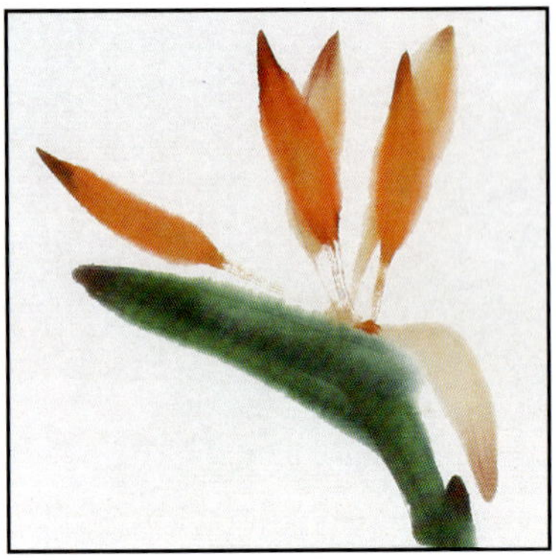

Dilute the mixed orange to a lighter tone and reload your brush as before. Now you add the remaining petals to the flower in such a way as they appear behind the first petals.

5.

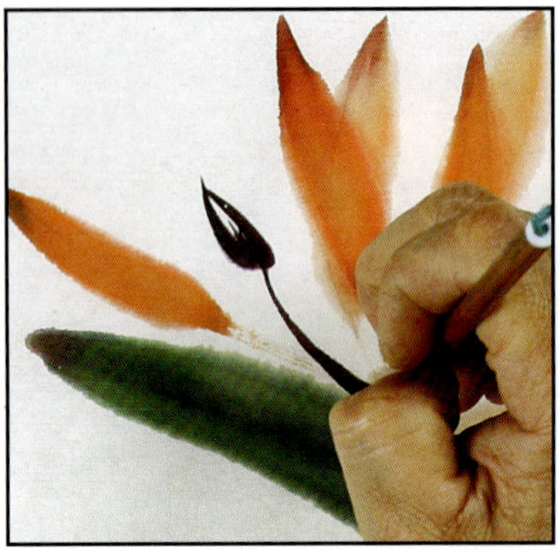

Finally, to complete the flower, add the stamen with your Vine brush. First mix the dark purple, using indigo and carmine, fully load your Vine brush with it, and tip the brush with indigo. The stamen is created in three strokes. The first two are downward strokes that hook in at the middle to join. Have each stroke curving outwards in opposite directions to leave the space in the middle. Join this to the center of the flower with the third stroke, pushing down gently towards the base of the petals. Add a small dot to the base of the stamen and your flower is complete.

6.

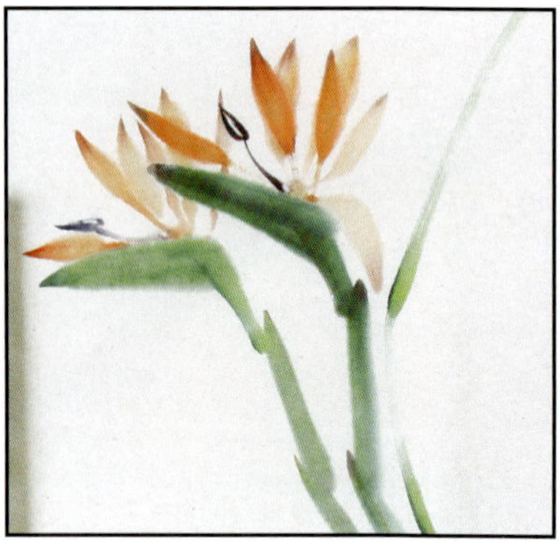

I use the same techniques to make a second flower. I paint it using more diluted tones of color so that it appears to recede into the background. Continue to add additional stems of flowers until you have as many in your composition as you wish. Be careful to not paint over the first flower — it should appear to be closer to the viewer and without other stems or petals crossing in front of it.

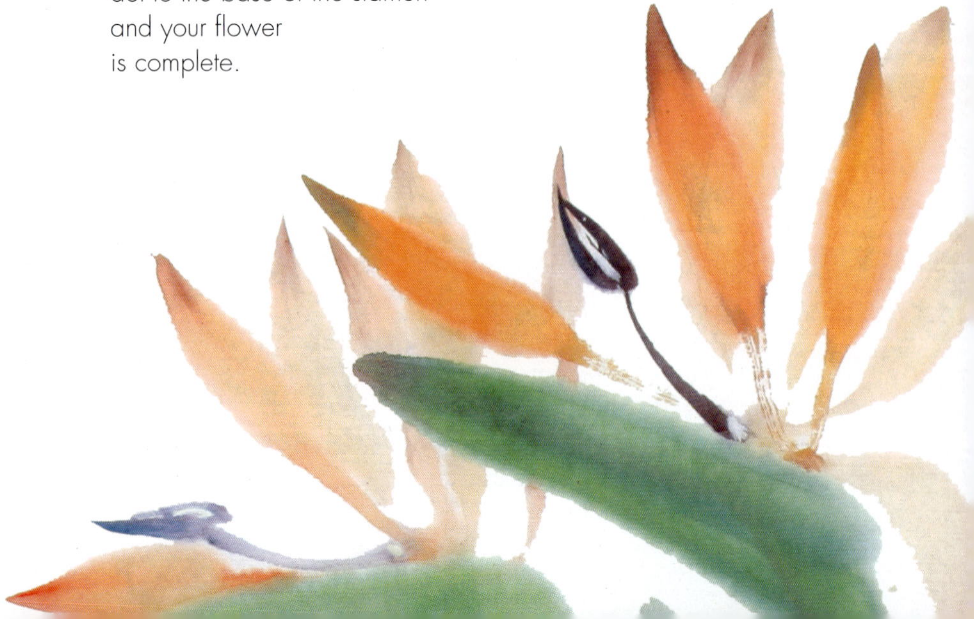

7.

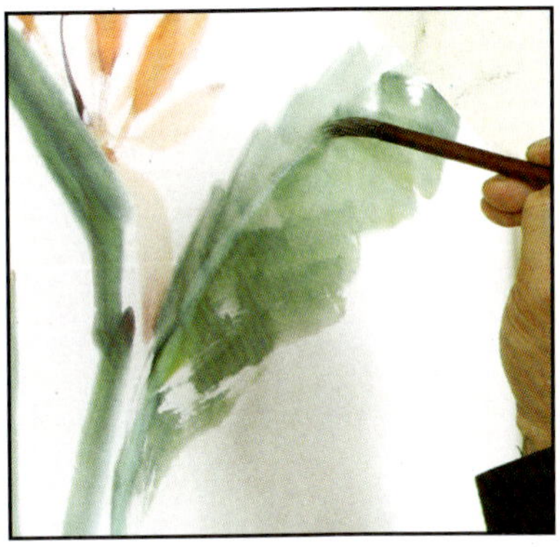

I paint the lighter of the large leaves first, the darker one in the forefront last. To paint in the leaves, use the Orchid Bamboo brush and mix a medium green from indigo and gamboge. Fully load the brush and paint the center stalk of the leaf, starting from the bottom of the page and sweeping upwards. Reload your brush and, starting from the top, use side strokes down the stem of the leaf to create the frond in choppy strokes. Repeat on the other side of the stalk.

8.

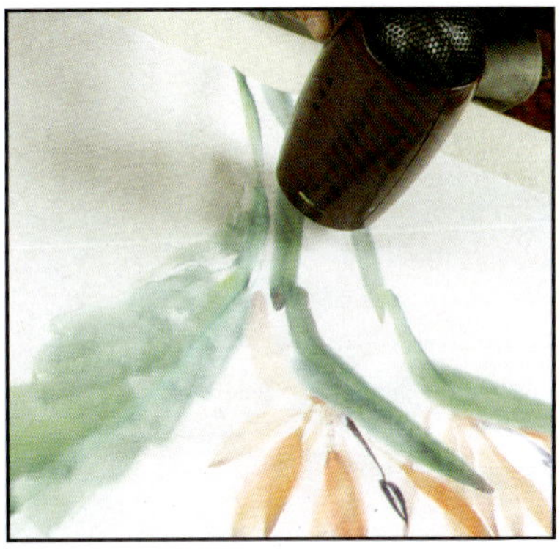

Before starting the darker leaf, I dry the first one with a hair dryer. Anytime you wish to paint one image over another without them bleeding into each other, you must allow the area to dry, and a hairdryer is a quick way of accomplishing this.

9.

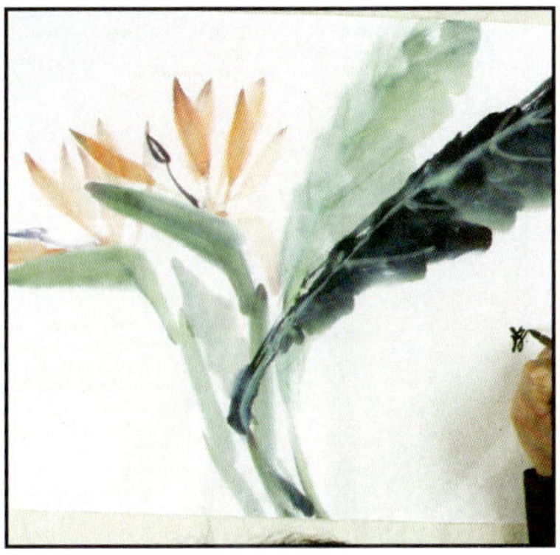

I paint in the second leaf overtop the first, using a darker tone of green. To create the veins of the leaves, I use an opaque green. Any paint can be made opaque with the addition of a white gouache or Chinese white. Mix a medium green and add a touch of the white. Using the Vine brush, paint in the veins of the leaves.

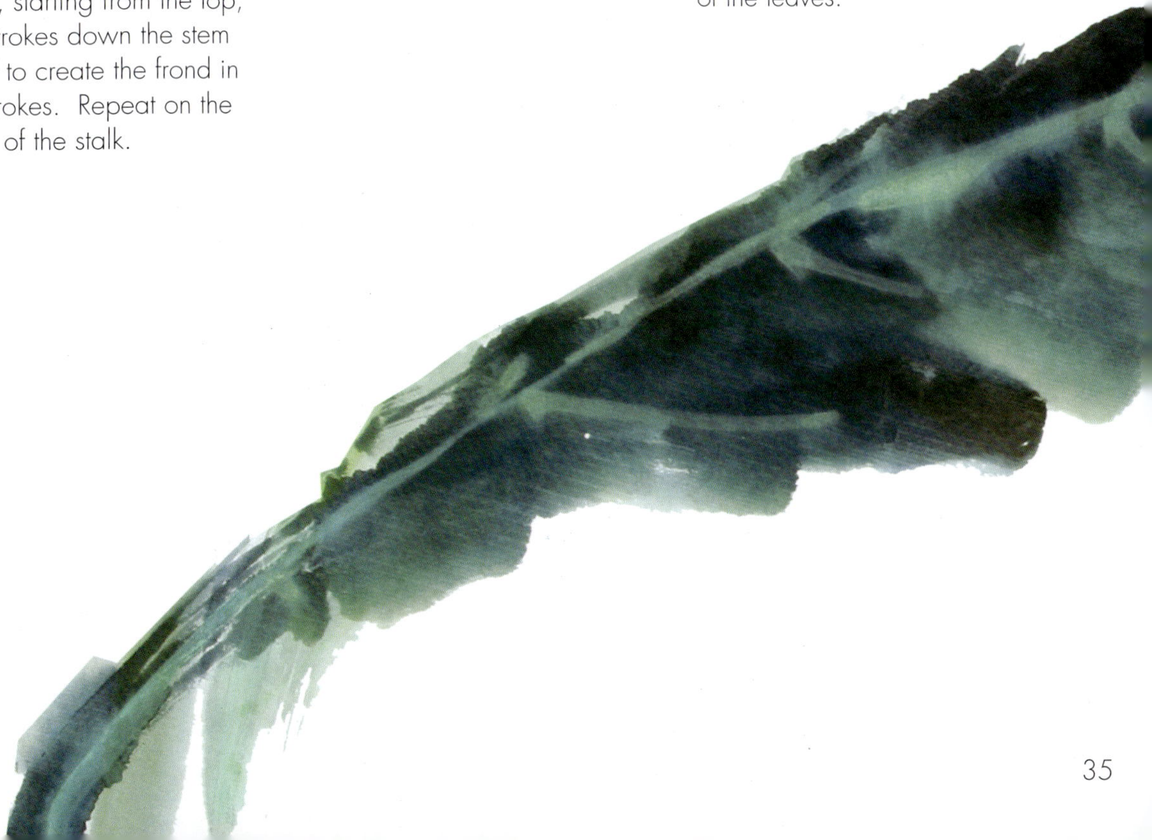

Butterfly with Tiger Lilies

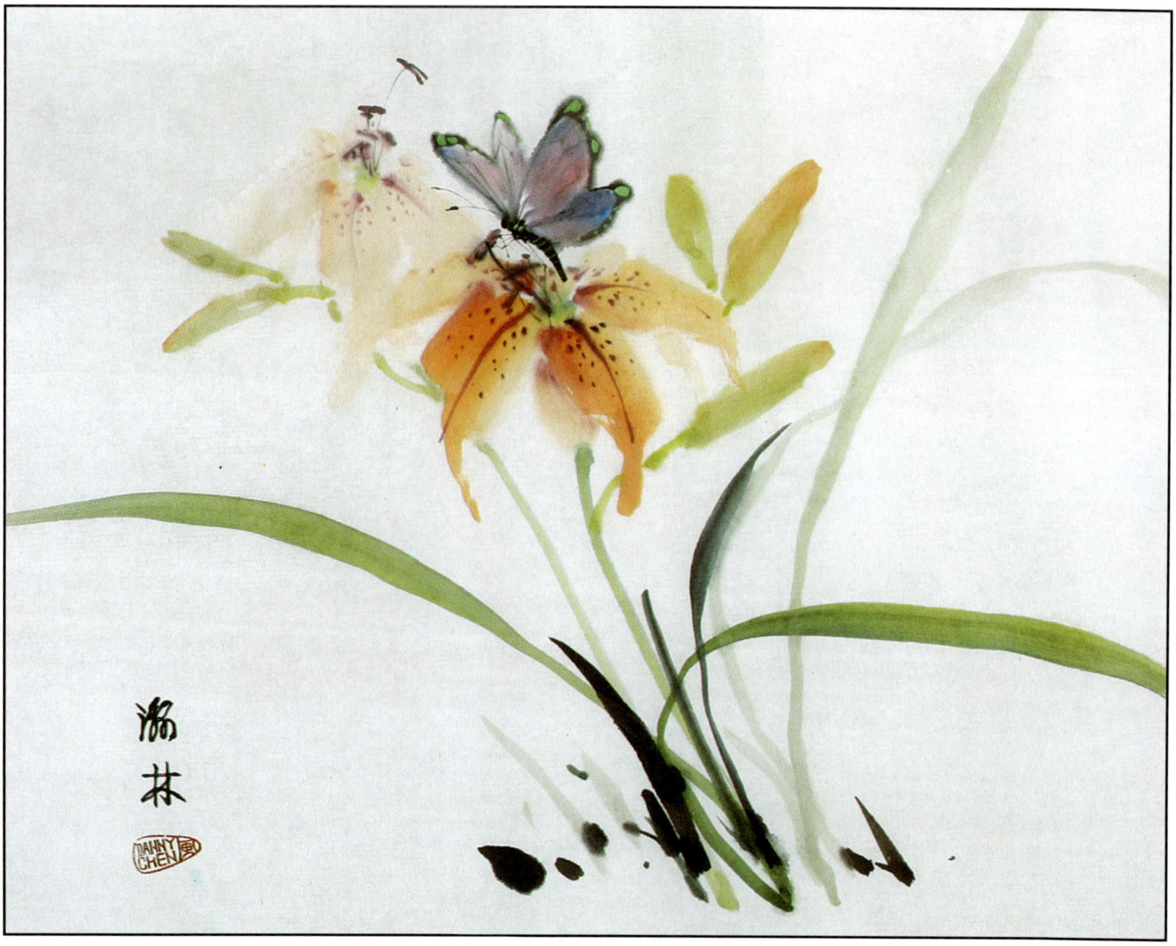

The butterfly is another interesting and fun demonstration because you can use your vision as an artist to create your own — there is no "right" or "wrong" way to form the wings, colors and patterns of a butterfly. Start to be expressive in your painting and let your own interpretation guide your brush. The tiger lily is a beautiful foil for the colors of this butterfly, however there is no reason you couldn't add an orchid, or bird of paradise instead.

1.

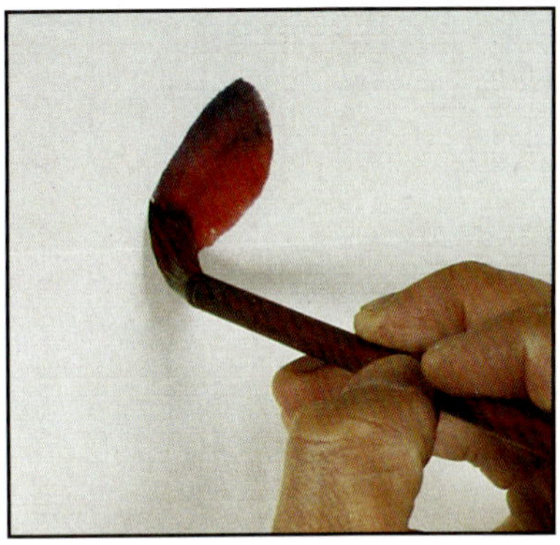

I first mix a purple using carmine and indigo, and then fully load my White Cloud brush with carmine, picking up the purple I just mixed half way, and then finally indigo on the tip. To create the main part of the wing closest to us, I use a sidestroke, pushing down without pulling the stroke at the end.

2.

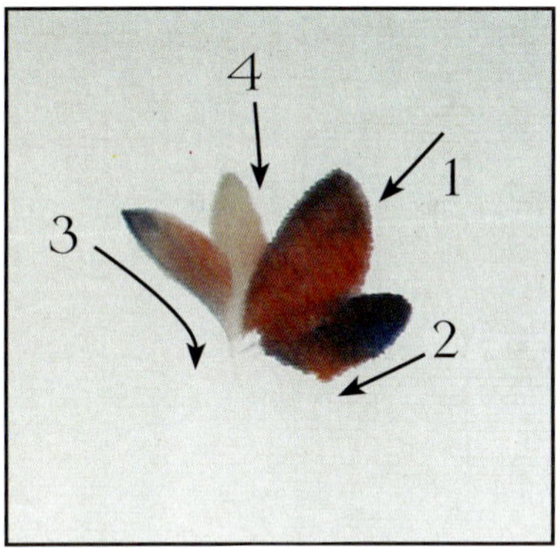

Finish the first wing by reloading your brush with the same mix and making a smaller side stroke, pushing towards where the body of the butterfly will be. Dilute the mix on your brush halfway with water, and then reload only indigo at the tip. Add in the third stroke, and without reloading your brush, finish the fourth stroke.

3.

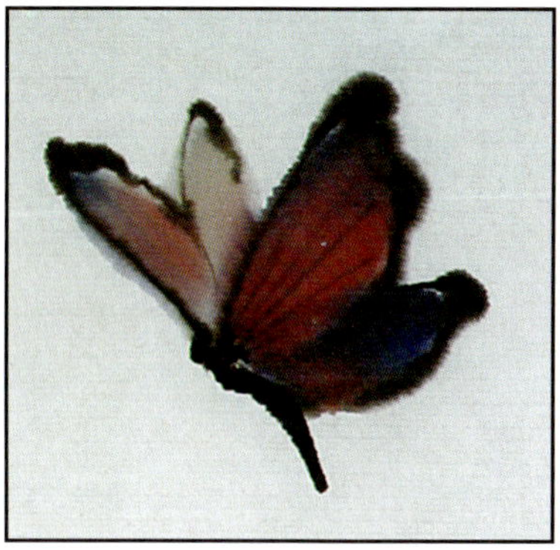

Use your Vine brush loaded with concentrated ink for the head, abdomen and body. The head is a short sidestroke — almost a small rectangle shape. The abdomen is made of two of the same stroke, but in a "V" shape, butting up to the head. Finally, the body is made in a sweeping stroke, starting at the tip of the tail and pulling upwards in a slight curve to join the abdomen. Still using a Vine brush and concentrated ink, outline the butterfly wings, bearing in mind the shape, pattern and texture of the wing. Be free to add as much or as little detail to create a unique look to your butterfly.

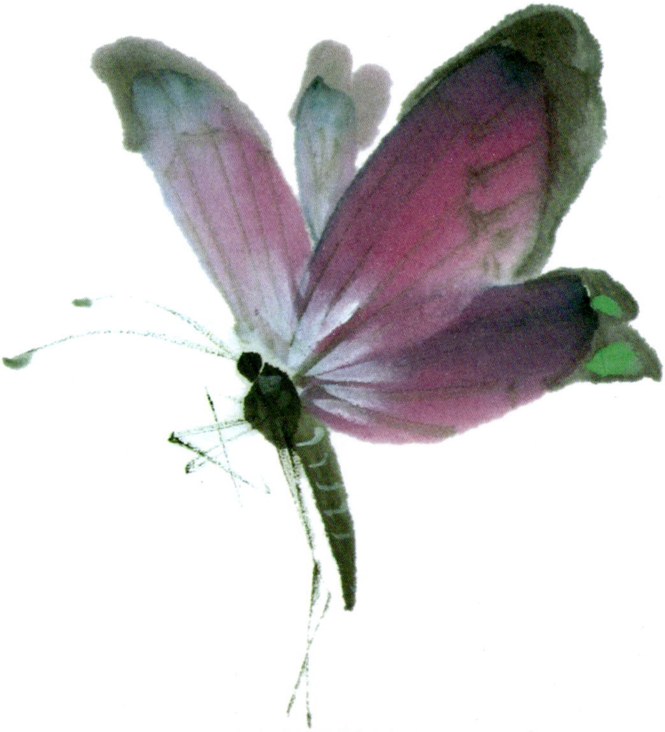

4.

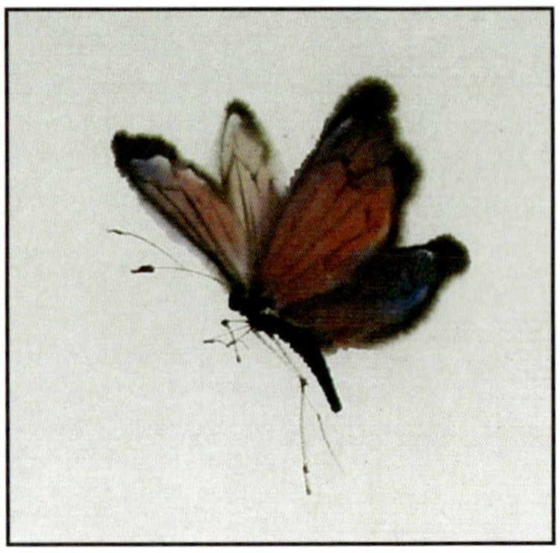

Using the Vine brush and concentrated ink, making sure that the tip of the bristles are in a sharp point, go ahead and add the legs, antennae and wing details. Use a light touch and swift strokes, and follow the image I've painted or adding what you wish to see. If you are having troubles mastering a thin line, practice on your pad first, varying the amounts of water, ink, pressure and speed of the stroke until you find the right touch.

5.

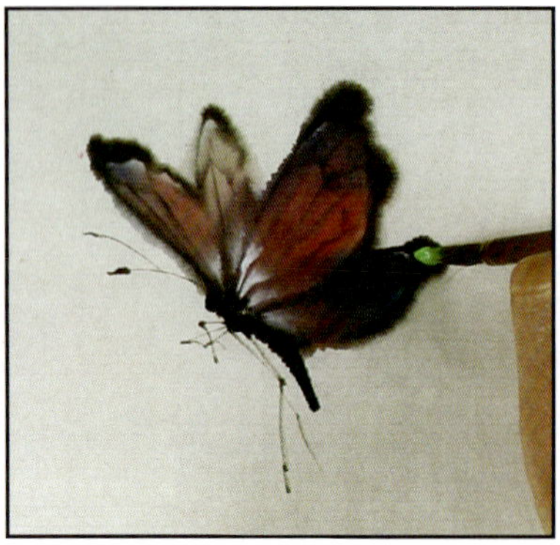

To finish your butterfly, add highlights, false "eye" spots and other color as you desire. Bear in mind, that if you wish to add one color overtop another, the top color needs to be opaque, or it won't show. I used a medium white and my Vine brush to press down small strokes with the tip pointing towards the body at the base of the wings to create the white highlights. I mixed a medium green with concentrated white to paint in the false eyes at the tip of the wings. Try yellow, turquoise, or other bright colors typical of the markings of a butterfly.

6.

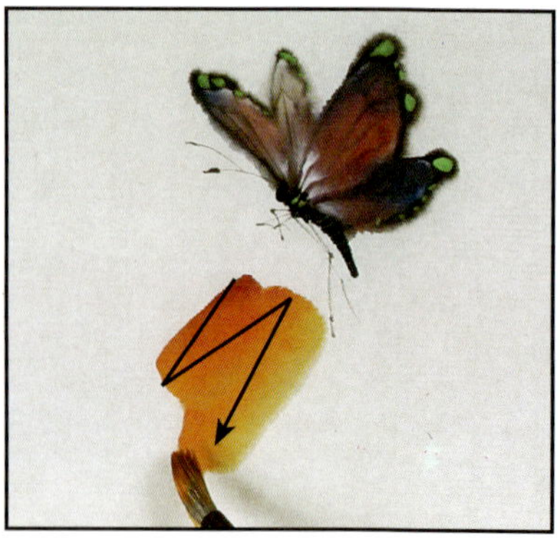

To create the tiger lily the butterfly is hovering over, I use my White Cloud brush to mix two different oranges. Use gamboge and carmine in different concentrations to create a lighter and a darker orange. To create the petals, load your brush with the lighter orange, then the darker orange halfway, and finally with carmine on the tip. Start your stroke by pushing the stroke down with the side of the brush, then pull up and push down a second stroke beside the first. Continue to push the stroke past where the first stroke ended, finally pulling the bristles straight down to create a "tail". Lift up at the end to taper the stroke, pulling your brush off the paper.

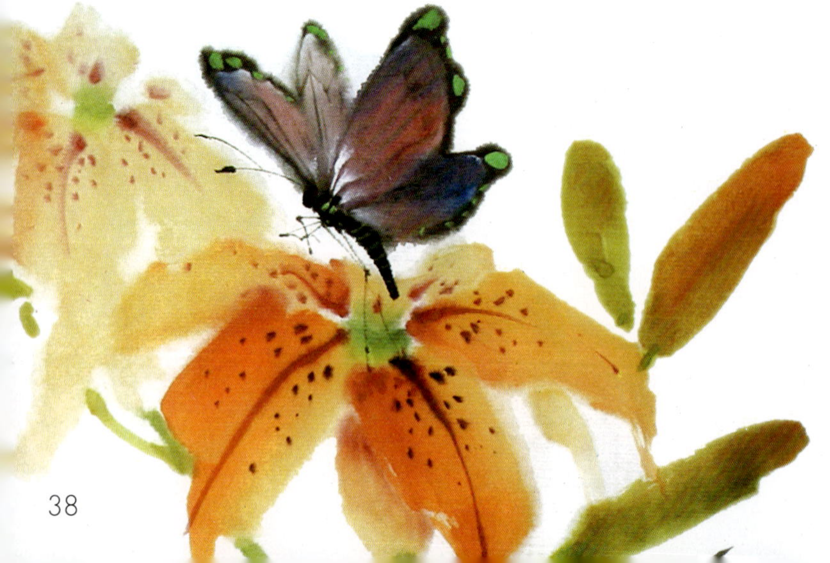

7.

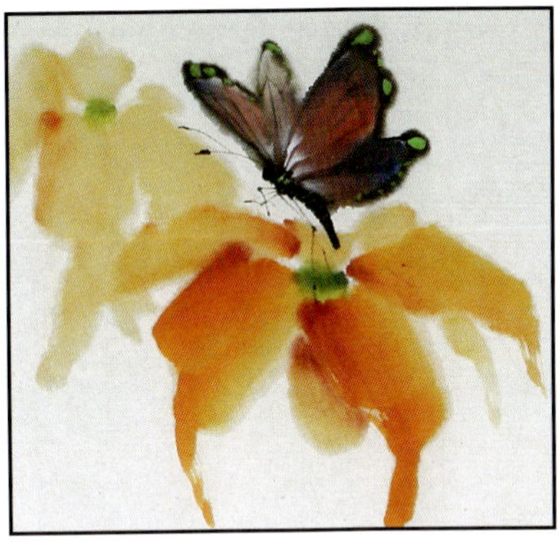

Create five petals in a similar fashion, watch the concentration of your paint and try to create tonal variation the way I did in the image above. For the center spot in the middle of the flower, pick up a light and a dark green and press down to create the oval shape. Finally, add the cup of the flower below the petals using the same mix of light orange, dark orange and carmine. Press down two strokes side by side from the top to the bottom of the cup. The strokes should be aligned with the center of the flower — directly underneath the green center spot you just added.

8.

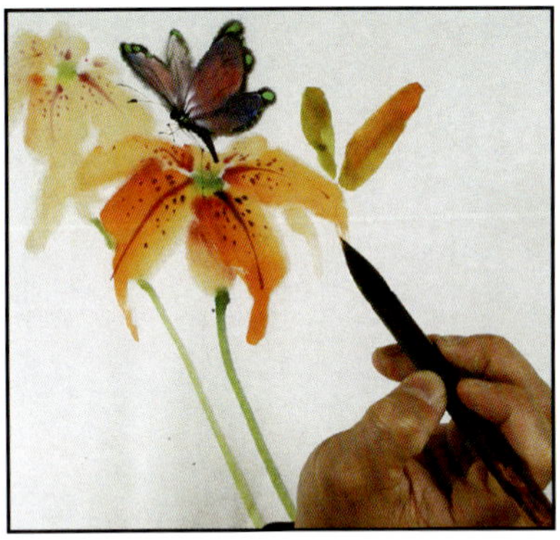

Finally, add the detail to the lily. Pick up carmine using a Vine brush, and create a nail head rat's tail stroke for the center vein of the petals. Continue adding spots, working from the center of the flower outwards to the tip of the petal. As you work, create progressively lighter and smaller spots along the length of the petal. Add stems to the flowers using the Orchid Bamboo brush. Load it fully with light green, adding dark green to the tip. Add the stems from the base of the cup, pulling down in a graceful sweeping stroke. Add the second stem without reloading the brush for a lighter tone.

9.

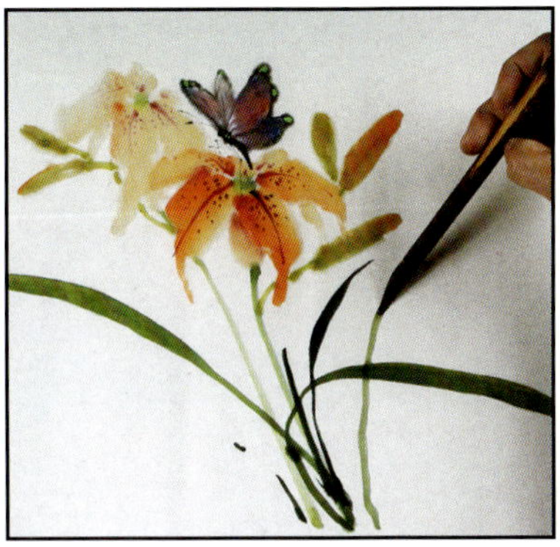

Add unopened lily buds by loading the Orchid Bamboo brush fully with light green and half with mixed orange. With two strokes, side by side, pull two strokes from the tip of the bud to the base. Reload light green for the second bud, using the same stroke, but shorter. I've added additional stems to join the flower buds and leaves using the same techniques I showed you in the Orchid demonstration. Feel free to add your own additional detail.

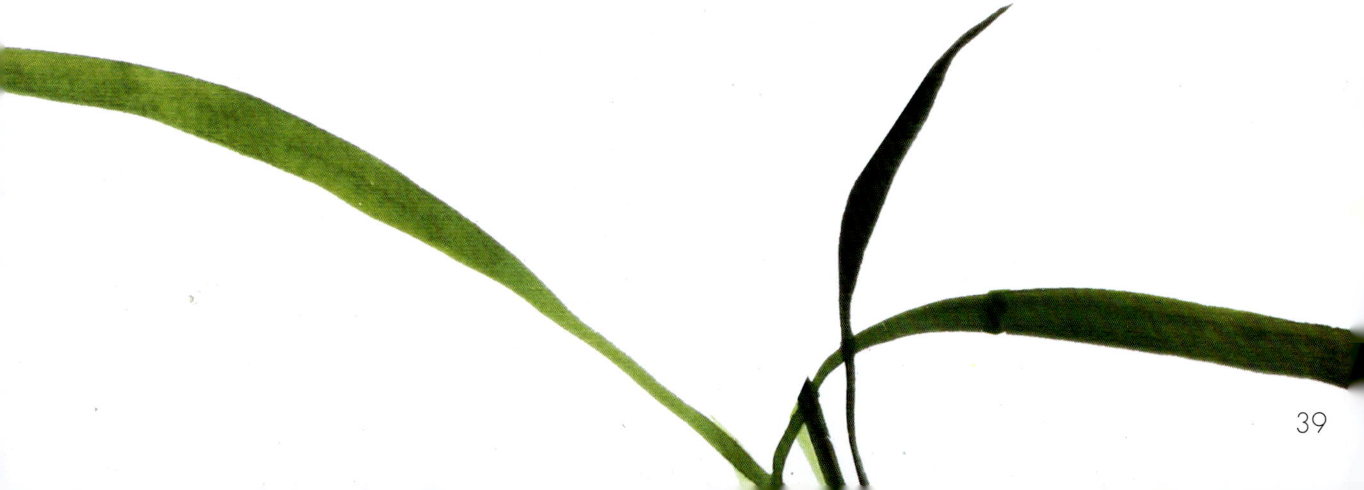

Dragonfly and Lotus

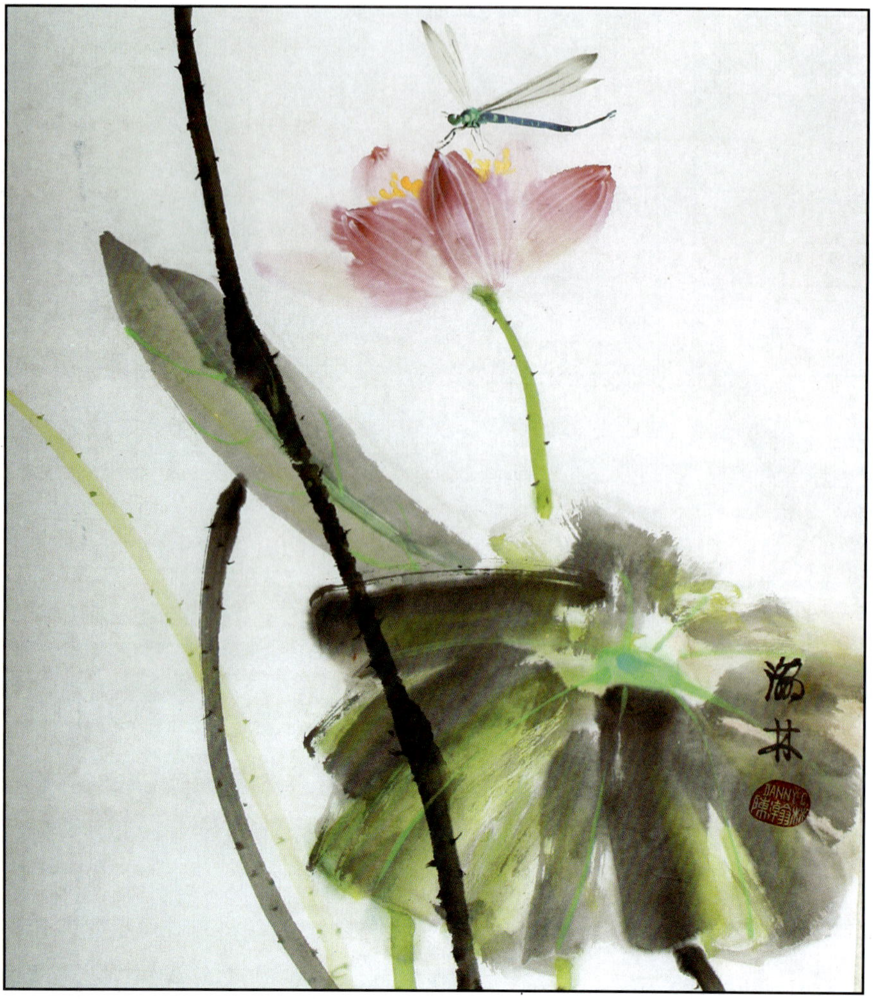

Although the lotus is a sacred flower in Buddhism, North Americans often confuse it with a water lily and lily pad, as there are similarities between the two flowers. A lotus leaf is broad and saucer-shaped the way a lily pad is, but is quite ruffled around the edges. It also does not rest on the surface of the water but will reach past it or even grow in mud and bogs. The flower is very delicate and is a symbol of faithfulness and purity.

1.

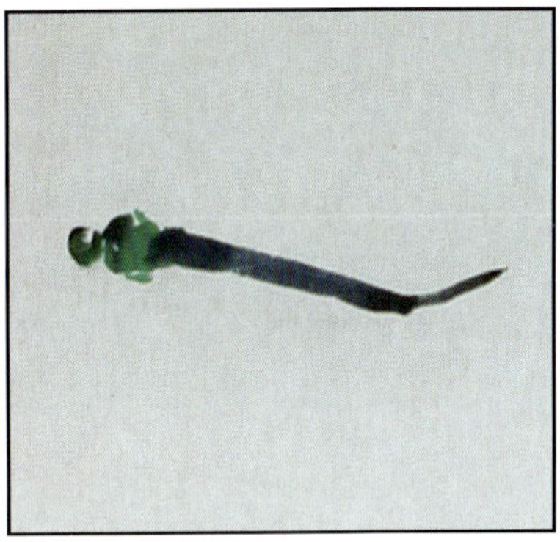

Load your Vine brush with dark green, and add indigo to the tip. Create the head of the dragonfly with a small circle, leaving a bit of white space if possible in the center for a highlight. Reload with the same mix for the abdomen and make two small strokes angling down and inwards to create a small "V", just touching up against the back of the head. Finally, for the body, reload the dark green and indigo and starting at the base of the abdomen (rather than the tip of the tail) pull straight back for the main length of the body, and then gently pull upward for the tail. Add a tiny second stroke at the very tip of the tail to splay it out.

2.

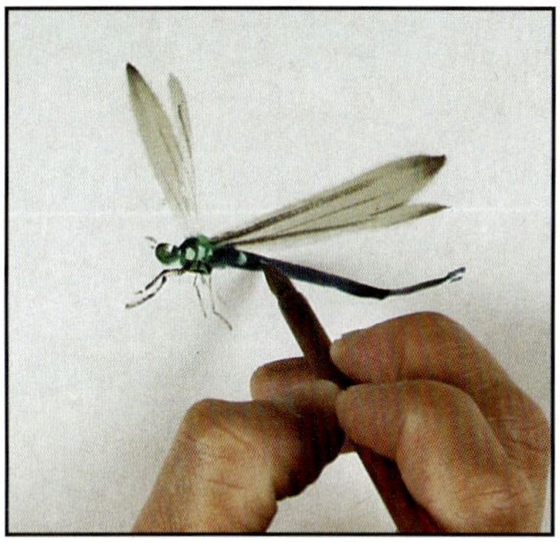

For the wings, use the White Cloud brush loaded fully with light ink, and then pick up dark ink at the tip. Start at the tip of the first section of wing, and pull down and towards the abdomen in a single stroke. Reload the dark ink and add the remaining wings using the same stroke. Load the Vine brush with concentrated ink and add in the details to the wings — again, trying to achieve a lacy, delicate look. Use a light hand to add the legs and antennae. Mix opaque green from medium green and concentrated white. Load this mix onto your Vine brush to add highlights onto the head, abdomen and body.

3.

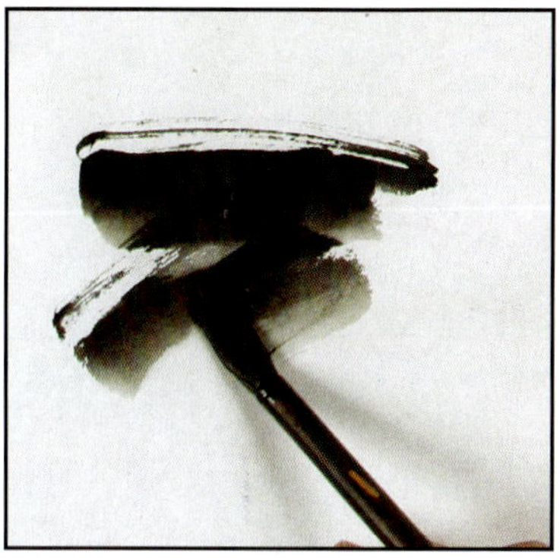

Load the Orchid Bamboo brush with medium ink, and then add concentrated ink to the tip. The stroke I use for this leaf requires that you have some fun, as it is very loose. Practice it on your pad first until you are comfortable with the movement. Use a side stroke, pushing down and pulling up 2 or 3 times in a zigzagging movement — finishing on the pull down, elongating and lifting at the end, the way you did in the tiger lily petal. Be strong with your strokes and use energy, transferring your chi onto your paper as you create the stroke. After practicing this a few times, go back to your composition and create the leaf using a number of these strokes, or even as a series of continuous zigzag strokes to create the oval shape. Use a combination of wet and dry brush strokes for interesting effect, and be spontaneous, letting your movements be free.

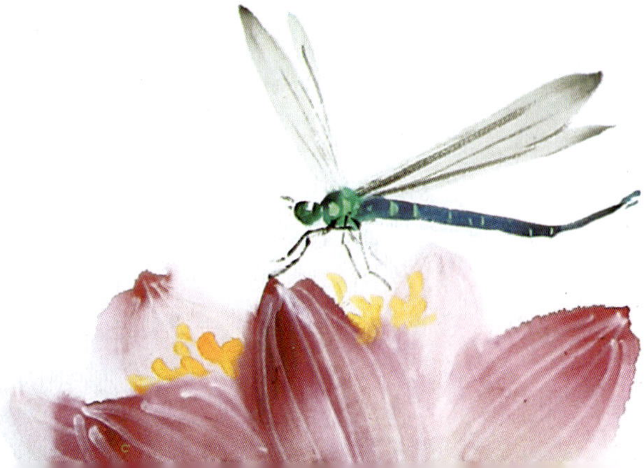

4.

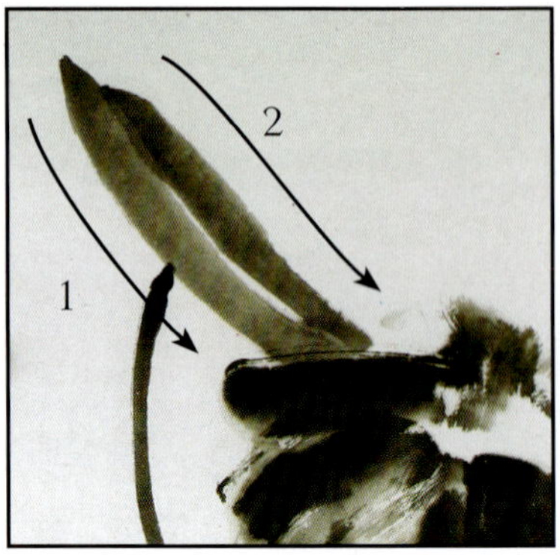

As with a lily pad, a young lotus leaf is curled up on itself, unfurling as it matures. Add an unopened leaf with light ink on your brush, and dark ink on the tip. In two strokes, from the tip of the leaf to the base, pull a long stroke downwards, pressing as you go to create a broad curving line. Try to leave a bit of white space in the between the two strokes, joining them at the start and end.

5.

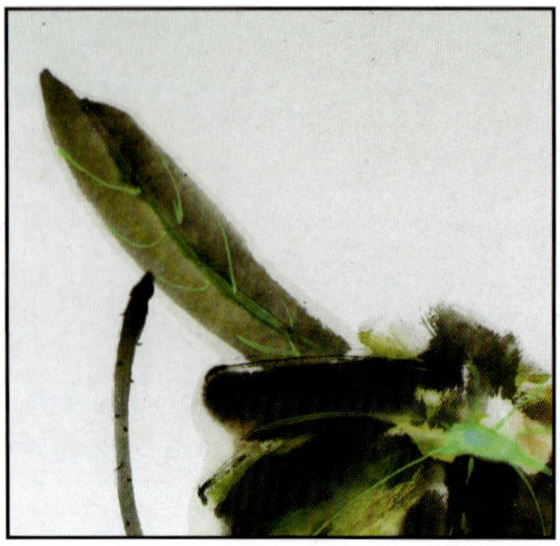

After the ink is dry, add color to your leaves by mixing a light green and fully loading your White Cloud brush. If you like, experiment with darker greens, add more yellow, or even add some burnt sienna to achieve a range of color in your leaves. Gently stroke the color over your leaves where the ink is lightest so that the color will show through. Use opaque green to add the veins and detail to the leaves, as well as the highlight in the center of the open leaf. Once you have added the leaves, review your composition. Because the leaves are a main focus in the painting and require so much space, I have added them before the flower. Now you can evaluate the best position for the flower to balance and improve your composition.

6.

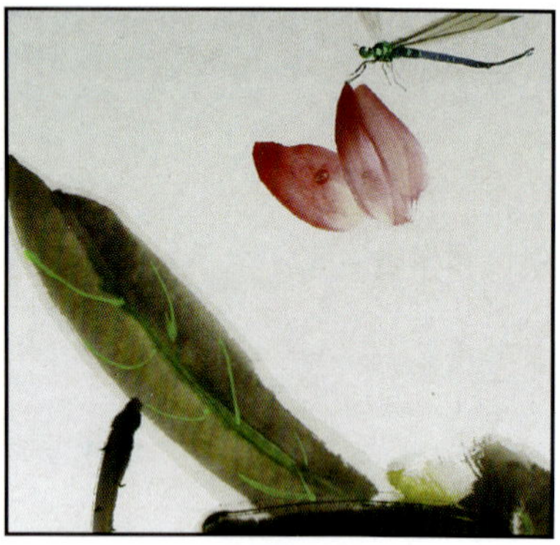

Start the lotus blossom by loading diluted carmine onto your Orchid Bamboo brush and concentrated carmine at the tip. Each petal is two strokes, created by touching the tip of the brush to the paper at the top of the petal, and pulling the stroke down — adding pressure through the center to widen it. Reload the concentrated carmine and place the second stroke beside the first to form the center petal. Continue in the same way, loading carmine to the tip of your brush to create the second and third petals at the center of the flower.

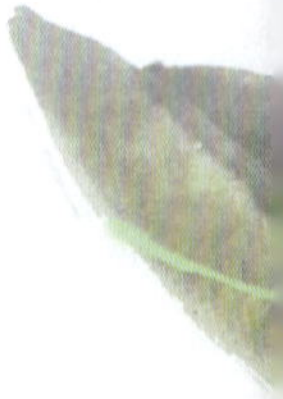

7.

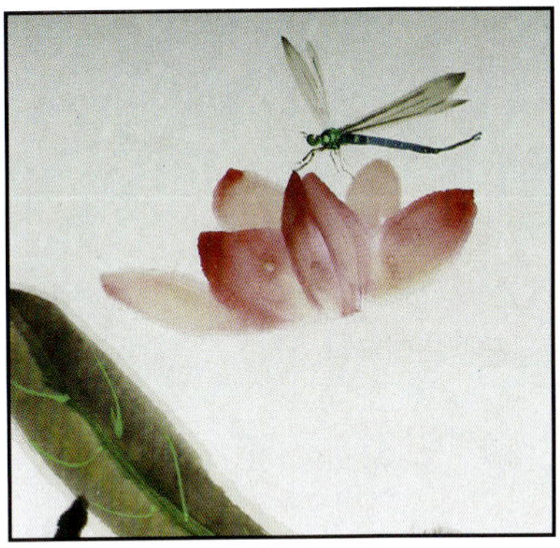

Dilute the carmine on your brush halfway and pick up concentrated carmine at the tip again to add petals toward the back of your flower. Fill out the flower with additional petals at the sides to balance the flower. Here I show six petals, a lotus blossom can have as many as twenty petals, depending on the variety, so add petals with your own eye to your composition.

8.

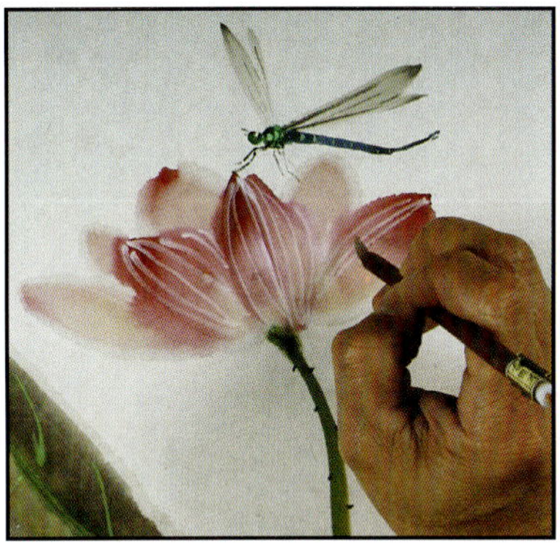

While the flower is drying slightly, add the stems to the painting. Use the stems to help you achieve a pleasing composition by breaking up the negative space. Negative space refers to the "blank" parts of the paper, and a technique for good design is to break this space into a number of smaller spaces of different sizes and shapes. This creates visual interest in your composition. To paint the stems, use your Orchid Bamboo brush loaded with varying tones of ink, green and burnt sienna as you wish. Don't forget to add the tiny thorns on the stems with your Vine brush while the stems are still damp. Finish your flower with your Vine brush and concentrated white to add in the nail head rat's tail stroke from the tip of the petals downwards, following the curve or contour of the each petal to create the detail.

9.

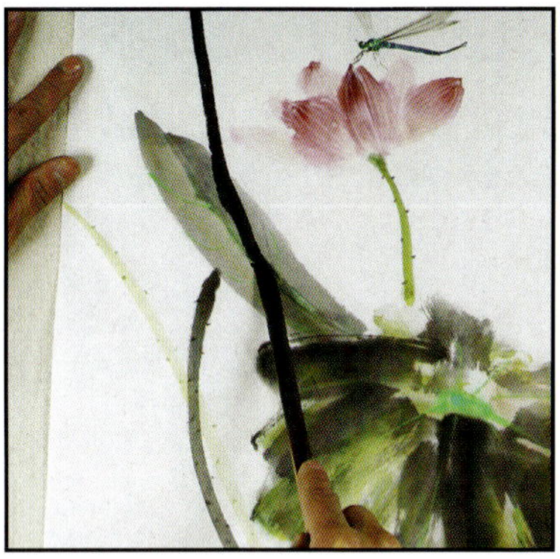

Finally, to add another plane to this composition and to create even further depth, I want to add a final stem in the foreground. However, to create this stem and to give it strength, notice how I hold the brush in a different way — transferring my chi from my body, through my arm and finally into the brush and onto the paper.

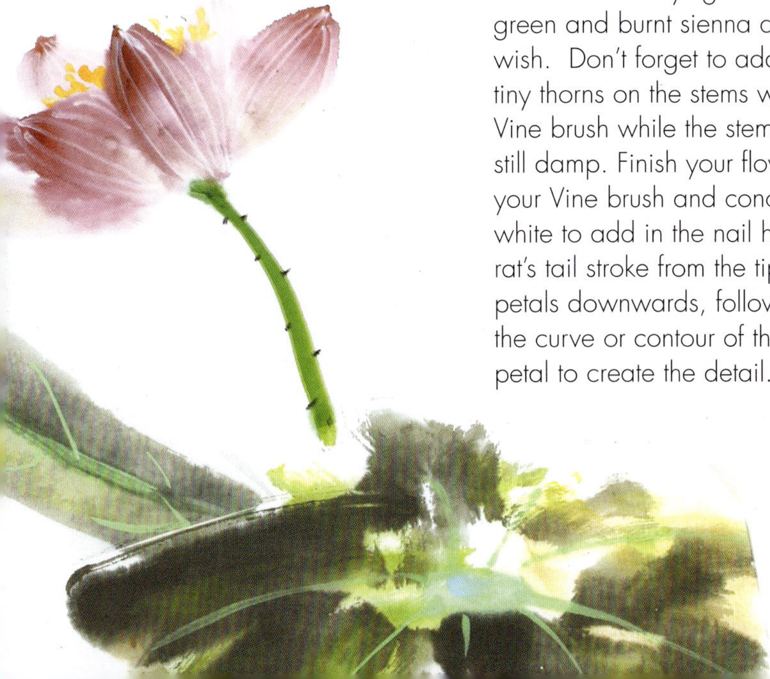

Grasshopper and Squash

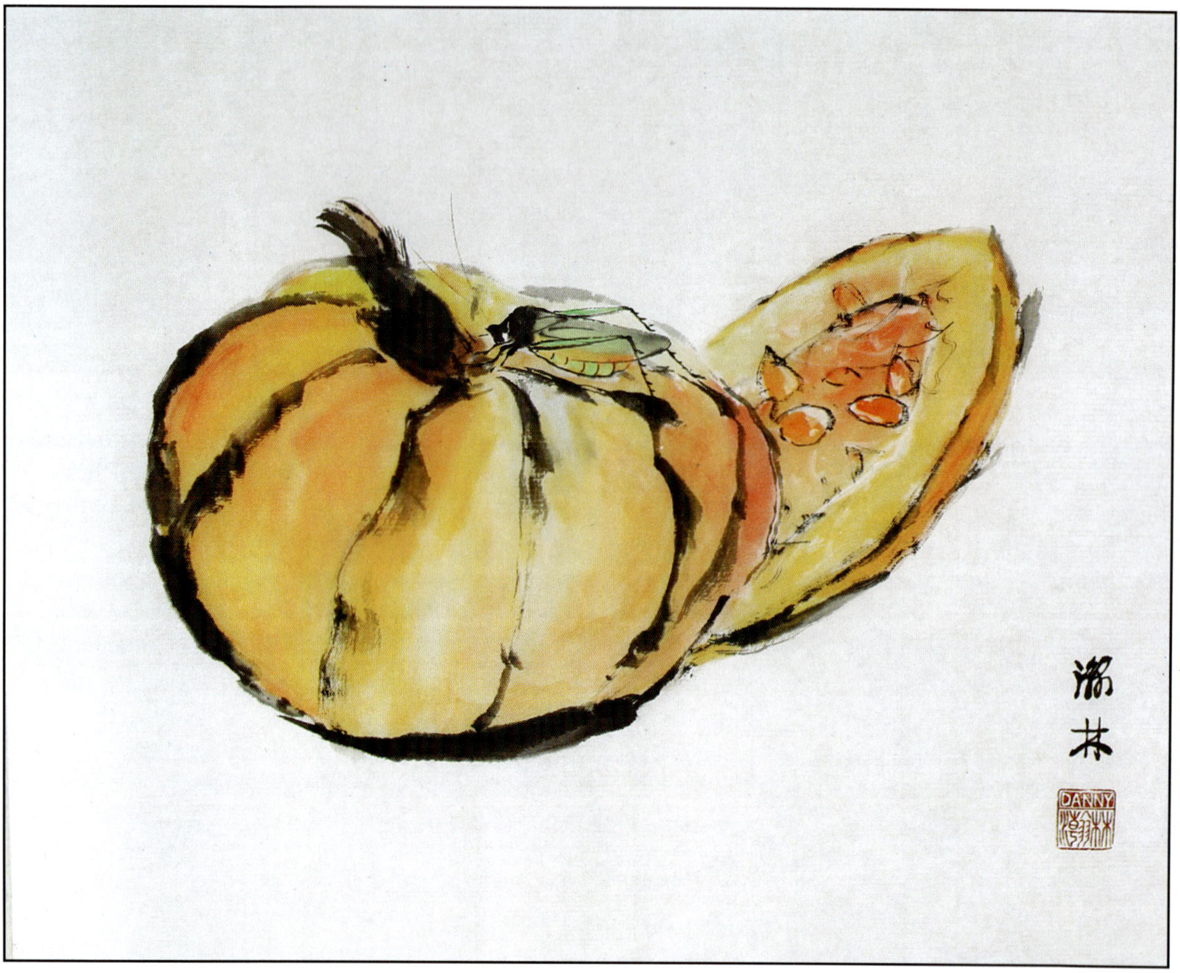

Chinese people believe that when a person dies, their soul will attach to an insect. This belief is strongly held and it is forbidden to kill any living insect so that the soul of the departed person may be protected. This demonstration shows a katydid (or grasshopper) on a pumpkin, perhaps taking a rest or perhaps watching over an ancestor's harvest!

1.

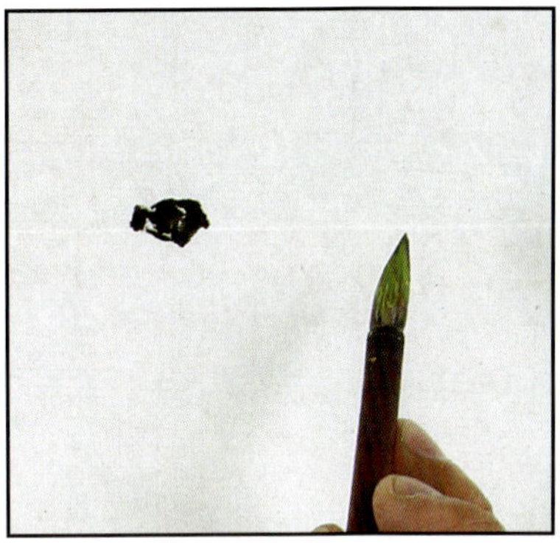

First, dip your White Cloud brush tip into concentrated black ink and touch it to the paper gently to form the head. Then quickly apply a second, smaller stroke for the neck. The thorax consists of four strokes to form a triangular shape that joins to the back of the head.

2.

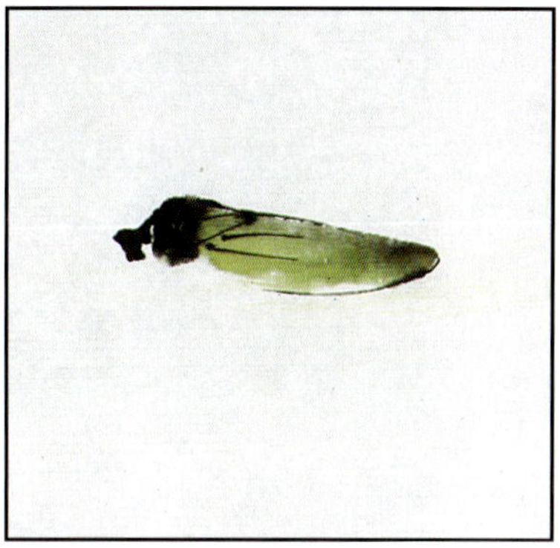

Next, load the whole brush with light green mix. Then load your brush with medium green then the tip with medium dark ink. This brush stroke is applied from the back end of the insect and moves toward the thorax, with the brush held at an angle while applying the paint to the paper. What you are aiming for is to produce a continuous gradient of color (from dark to light green) that reflects the natural variation in the color of the wing. Using medium-dark ink, draw in the texture of the wing with your Vine brush following this illustration.

3.

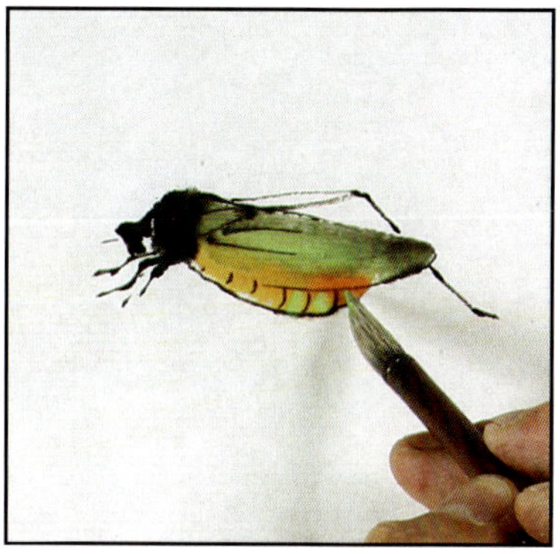

For the abdomen first fully load the White Cloud brush well with light green and pick up some burnt sienna with half of the loaded brush head. Try to lay down one sweeping stroke that has a slight curve to it extending almost from the back end of the wing to the lower part of the thorax. With medium-dark ink on the Vine brush, we can create the divisions visible in the abdomen of the insect. Next, we coat part of the wing and body with a green paint mixed with a little white to harmonize the color of the wing and the body and create an element of depth.

4.

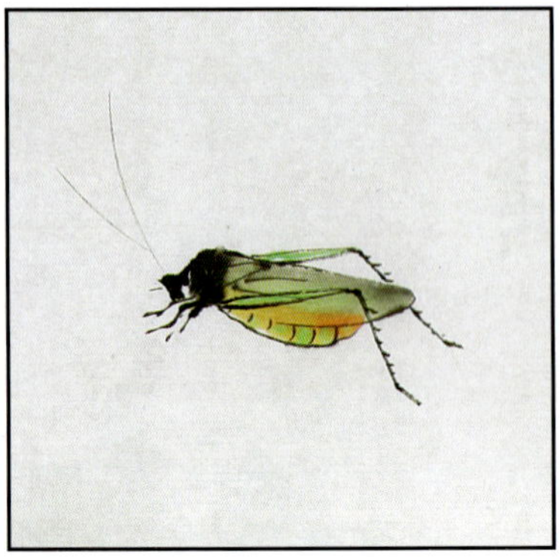

Finish up katydid's wing and hind leg using a Vine brush and a steady hand, drawing in the legs. Notice that a katydid's hind leg is quite long with tiny spike-like projections. I always encourage my students to observe a subject carefully and closely follow the form and shape of that subject for accuracy. As an artist, once we are familiar with the subject, we no longer merely reproduce the appearance of the subject but aim to convey the essence or spirit of the subject. Sometimes we choose to eliminate, exaggerate or even create certain details to express what we see and "feel". Finally, we finish by applying feelers with the Vine brush and the lightest of strokes. You may need to practice a few times before drawing it onto the actual painting to ensure that the angle, relative intensity and the length of the feeler is proportionate and delicate looking.

5.

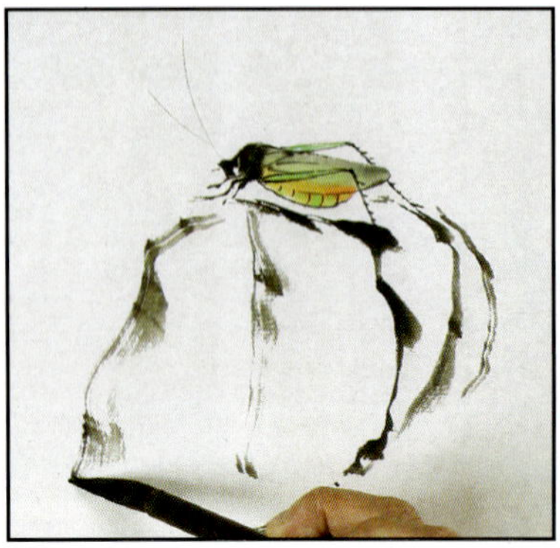

Move on to the squash. Use the Orchid Bamboo brush loaded with concentrated ink, but quite dry. After loading the brush, use a paper towel to wipe away some of the ink and to press the bristles down and twisting to splay them open slightly. Use your brush in this way to paint in a rough, loose outline of the pumpkin ensuring that the katydid winds up positioned on its surface.

6.

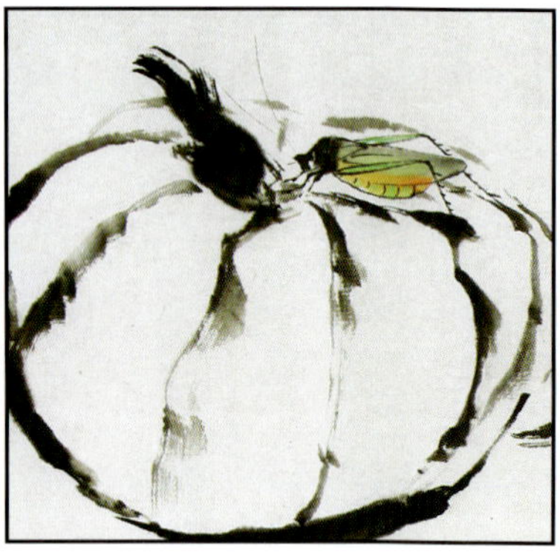

I retrace some of the lines with darker ink, to give depth and weight to the pumpkin. In Chinese brush painting, traditionally light and shadow is not discussed or given much emphasis. Often the subject was studied in a natural setting, and then painted in the studio with simple supplies and techniques. Capturing the spirit or essence of the subject, rather than the technical aspects of the subject. Today we are accustomed to the western style of art where light and shadow are an important part of representing the subject "accurately" and as such I give the impression of shadow as well, by using heavier lines and darker tones where shadow would normally be cast. To finish with the stem, pick up dark ink

7.

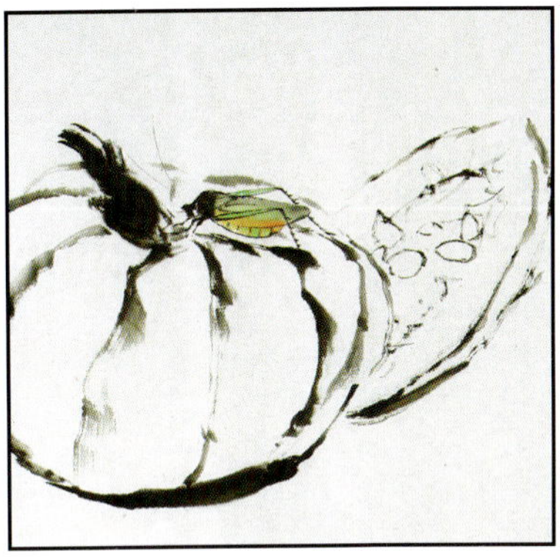

on your brush, but be aggressive in wiping much of it off and splaying the bristles of the brush open. Pick up more ink on the tip of the brush, and using an abrupt motion and chi, add in the woody stem with a short jabbing stroke. Outline the half pumpkin in the same way you did the first, adding the darker strokes where the shadows would lay.

8.

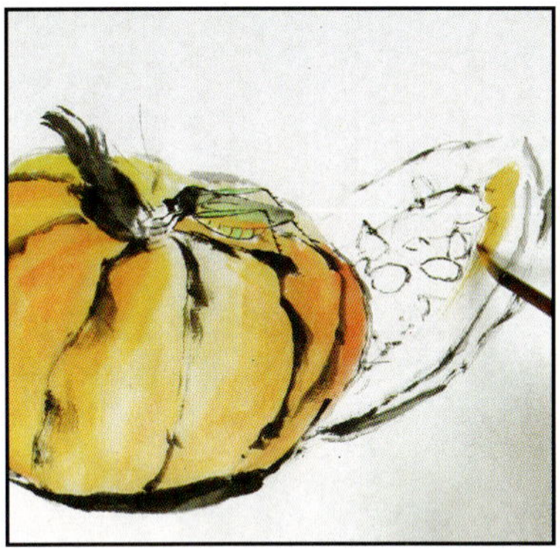

Use various mixed orange tones on your White Cloud brush to fill in your pumpkin. Again, think about where the light would hit the squash and use lighter tones in these areas. As you are working with the orange, be sure to remix your color every time you load your brush. By doing this each time, you load a subtly different tone on your brush and this gives depth and richness to the shell of the pumpkin. If you pick up the same color each time, your pumpkin will have a flat appearance overall.

9.

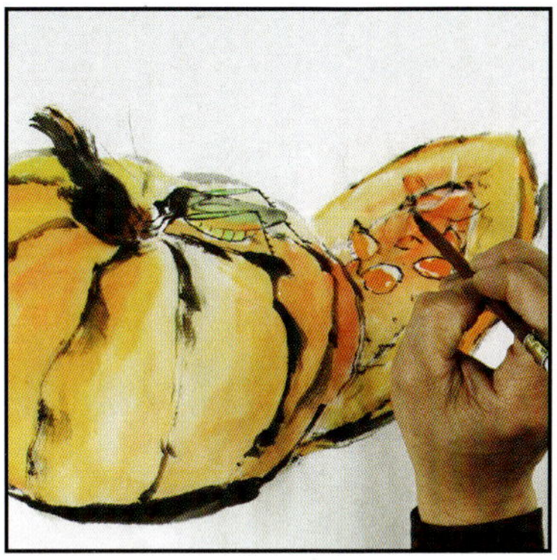

To finish the inside of the open pumpkin, I use a Vine brush and concentrated white to highlight the seeds and the inner rim. I splay the bristles and use loose, wiggly strokes around the inside of the pumpkin to remind us of the stringy fibers that are typical of a squash. I then added similar strokes again but with ink.

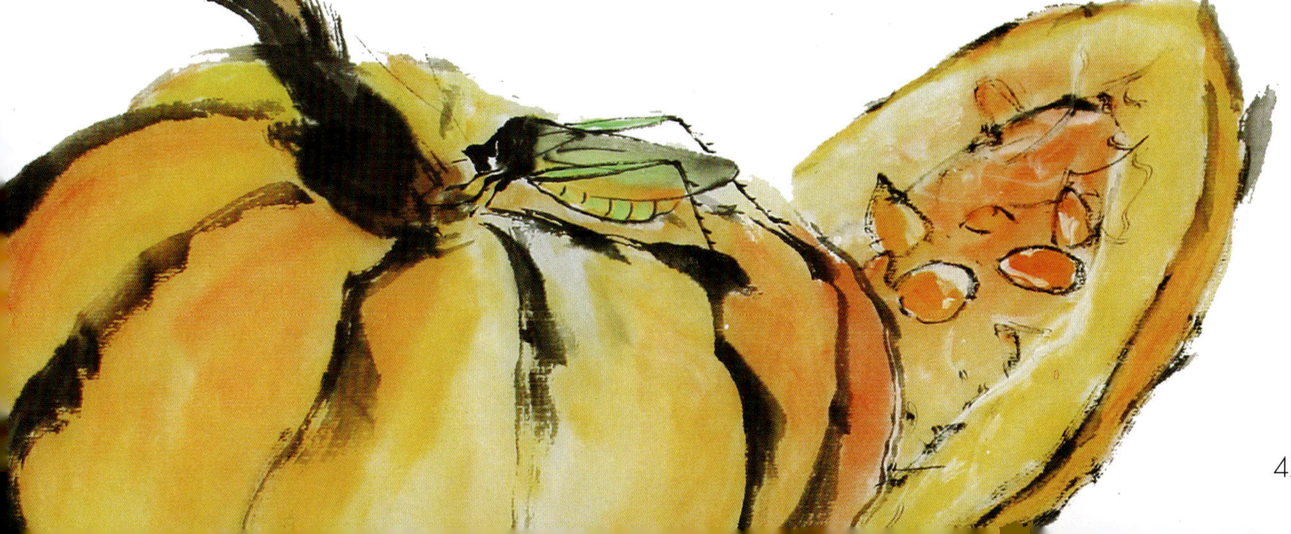

CHICKADEE AND IVY

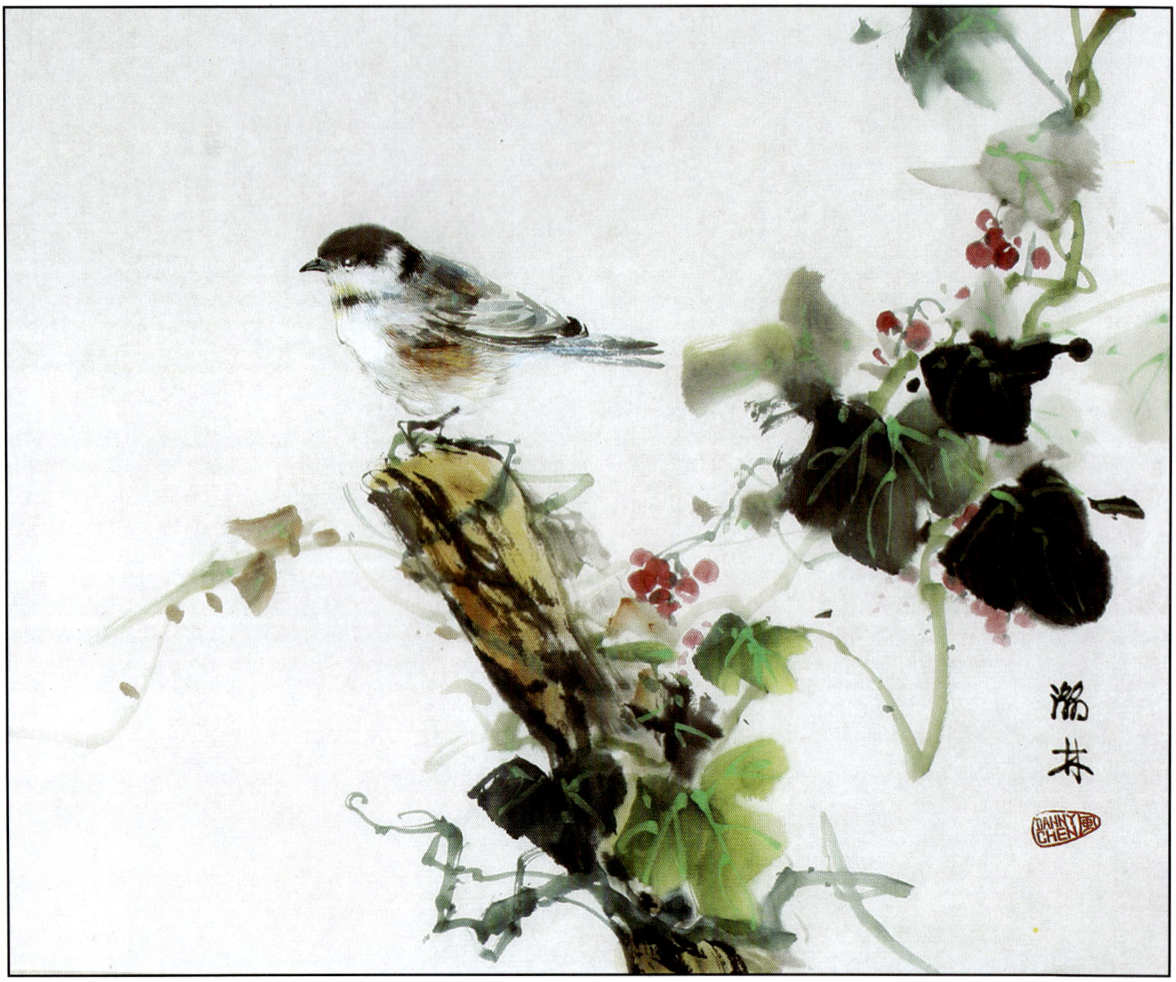

As mentioned in the previous demonstration, it is imperative that an artist studies his subject in detail to learn form and accuracy. Although many of us see birds every day, when called upon to draw their basic shape from memory, most of us would find this difficult. The next time you stand on your balcony, at a window or in your yard, take a moment to pay close attention to the birds and notice their wings, color and shape of their feathers, and how they stand. Take a snapshot to refer back to while you are painting if you find this helps. I have chosen a chickadee for this demonstration as it is very common in North America and many of us will have an opportunity to study one up close.

1.

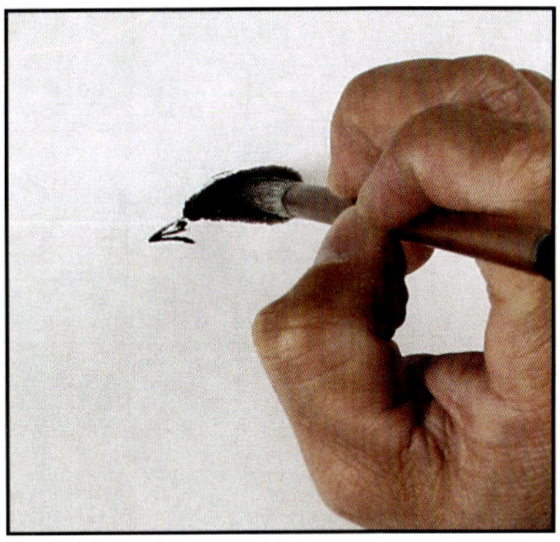

Pick up medium ink on a White Cloud brush, and add concentrated ink to the tip. Begin by painting the cap of the chickadee by pulling a small stroke and gently pressing up slightly. Done properly, the ink from the bristles will bleed upwards into the xuan paper creating a soft, feathery cap for the bird. Use your Vine brush and concentrated ink to paint three small nail head rat's tail strokes to create the beak. Each stroke should curve slightly to create the beak shape, and finish with a small dot for the nostril.

2.

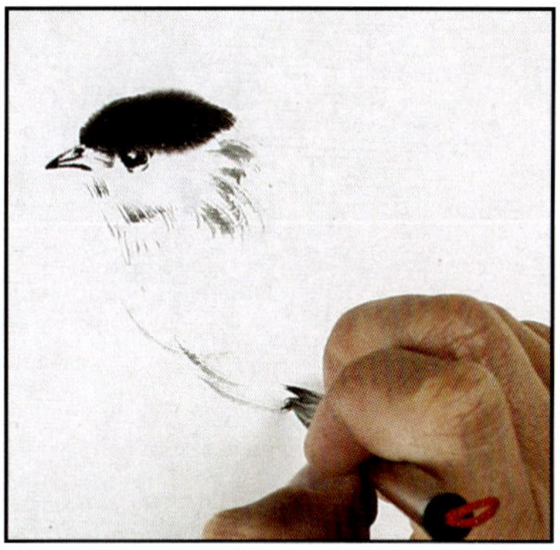

The eye is made with a half circle using your Vine brush and concentrated ink. Make the half circle slightly smaller than you need, as the ink will bleed outwards. Next pick up light ink on your brush and indigo on the tip. Splay the bristles and gently brush in tiny feathers to give shape to the head and throat areas. Continue to the back of the head. Then, loading the same mix on an open brush, come into the chest area and continue adding feathers with soft, light strokes to give the general chest shape.

3.

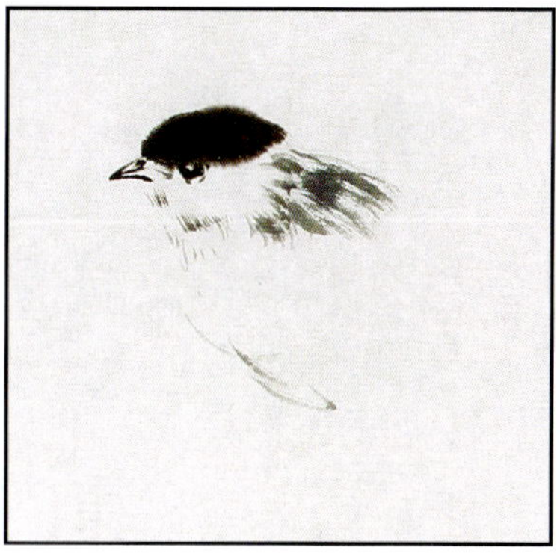

With your Vine brush, now pick up light indigo with medium ink at the tip. From the back of the neck, add feathers to create the shape of the bird with small, short strokes. Press down for each stroke and then pull up, creating a stroke that is broad at the base but tapers and becomes wispy at the tip. This creates the look of the individual feathers. Go back with your Vine brush and picking up more indigo, dry the brush and splay the bristles again. Gently brush over your strokes to continue to add soft layers of feathers.

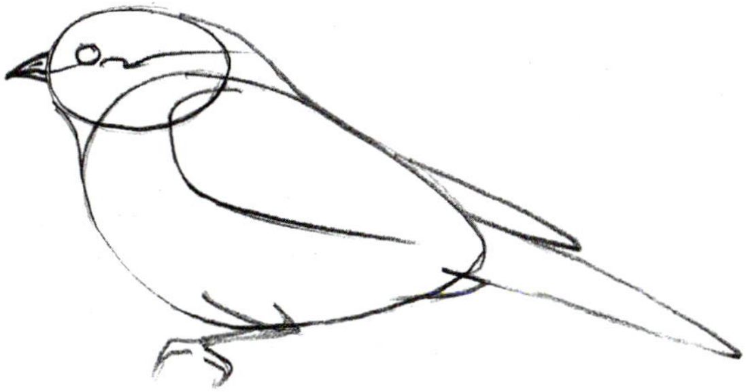

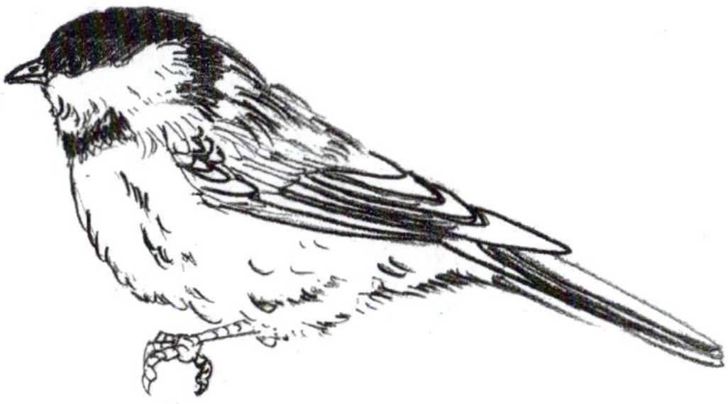

4.

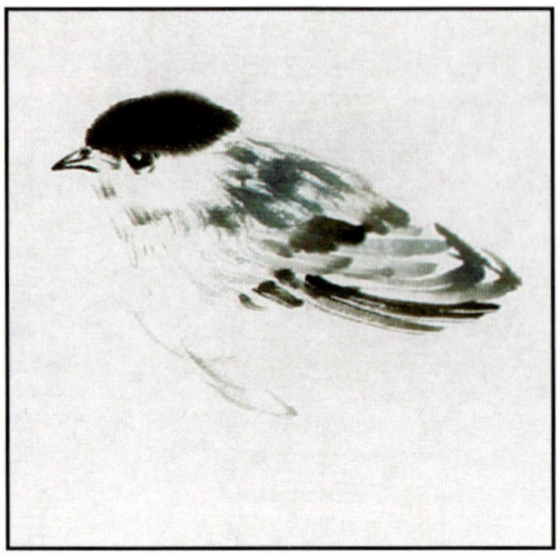

Use your Vine brush to fill in any other details that you think you need to flesh out the features of the chickadee. Remember to leave some paper white in the hollow of the bird's eyes to indicate the reflection of light and to create the illusion of life.

5.

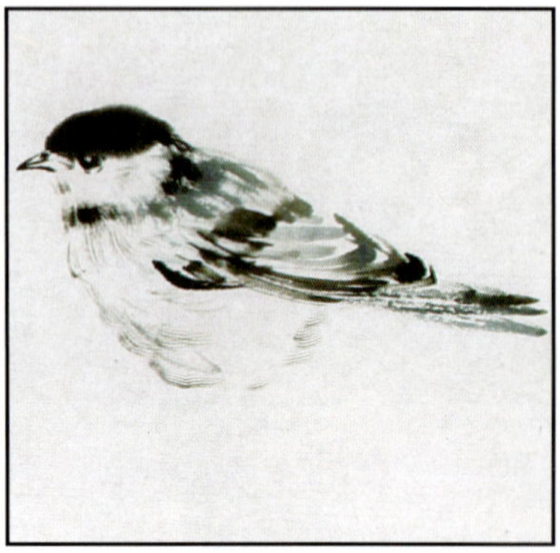

Pick up more ink and continue filling in the back of the chickadee. As you reach the wing area the strokes become progressively longer. Imagine the wing of a bird as you do this to help you create the strokes, and practice on sketch paper until you achieve the results you like. You can then use your sketch underneath the xuan paper as a guide to trace while you paint. Continue with an open, fairly dry brush with indigo and light ink to finish the chest and tummy of the bird. The tail feathers are made in the same way as the wing feathers, using the Vine brush fully loaded with medium indigo and tipped with ink. Use long strokes for the tail, pulling up at the end.

6.

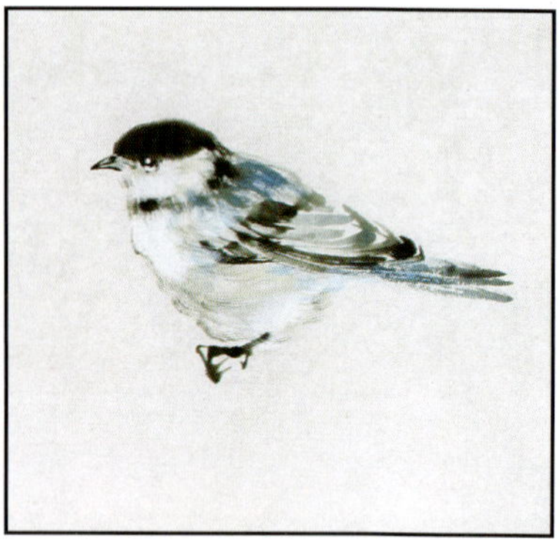

Wait for your painting to dry before continuing on to add in the color. Use light indigo and the White Cloud brush to fill in the back, following the line of the body. Pick up medium white next to brush in feathers around the face and the chest. Add highlights to the back and tummy as well. To finish the highlights and make the white pop out, go over the medium white strokes you just made again, but with concentrated white. Add a small white dot to the eye for the reflection. Finally, finish your bird by painting in the legs. Use your Vine brush and the nail head rat's tail stroke and a light hand to add in the leg. Be careful not to have too wet a brush or the ink will bleed and you will end up with a big foot!

7.

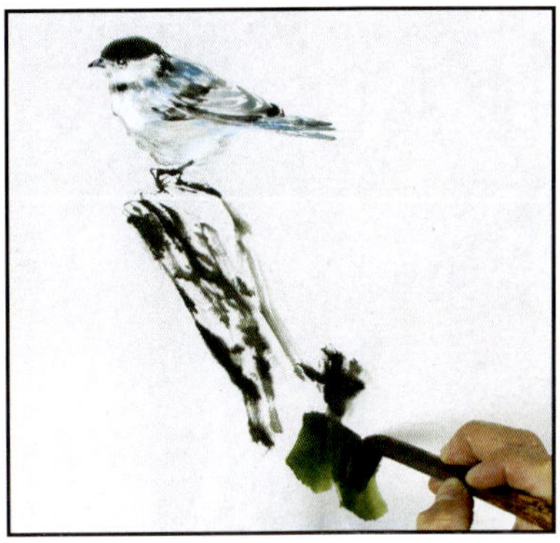

To add the trunk, use your Orchid Bamboo brush loaded with medium ink and the tip with dark ink. Dry the brush a bit on a towel, separating the bristles to achieve a dry look for the bark on the trunk. Make random strokes, keeping in mind the shape and feel of the trunk. Start at the base of the chickadee leg and work downwards. Then, to start the vine, use your Orchid Bamboo brush to mix light green and dark green. Load your brush with these and then add ink to the tip. A full leaf can be made by pushing and pulling a series of small side strokes, much in the same way as you mad the lotus leaf. As you work up the vine, randomly change the tone of your color and even the size and strength of your strokes to reflect the changing color of foliage in nature.

8.

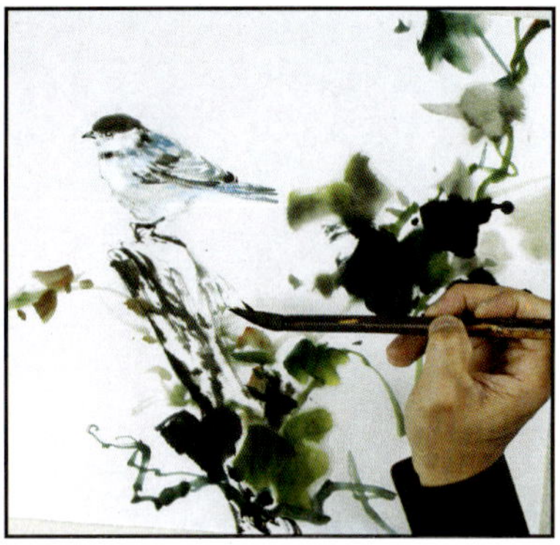

Complete most of the leaves, notice how some of mine are no more than "blotches" and are many colors. Join the ivy leaves to the vine using the Orchid Bamboo brush and a series of nail head rat's tail strokes, making some thick and some thinner. Ivy is a wild, unruly climber, so use randomness in your strokes to help you achieve this feeling.

9.

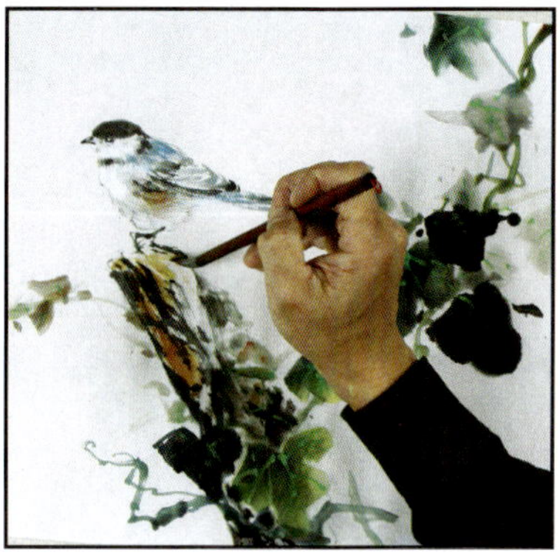

Use your White Cloud brush and burnt sienna to fill color in the trunk. Reload your brush, splaying the bristles to add a final touch of color in the wing area of the bird. Look at the overall composition and add more "blotches" in burnt sienna for the leaves to balance the painting. Final detail is added with carmine berries and opaque green for the veins in the leaf detail.

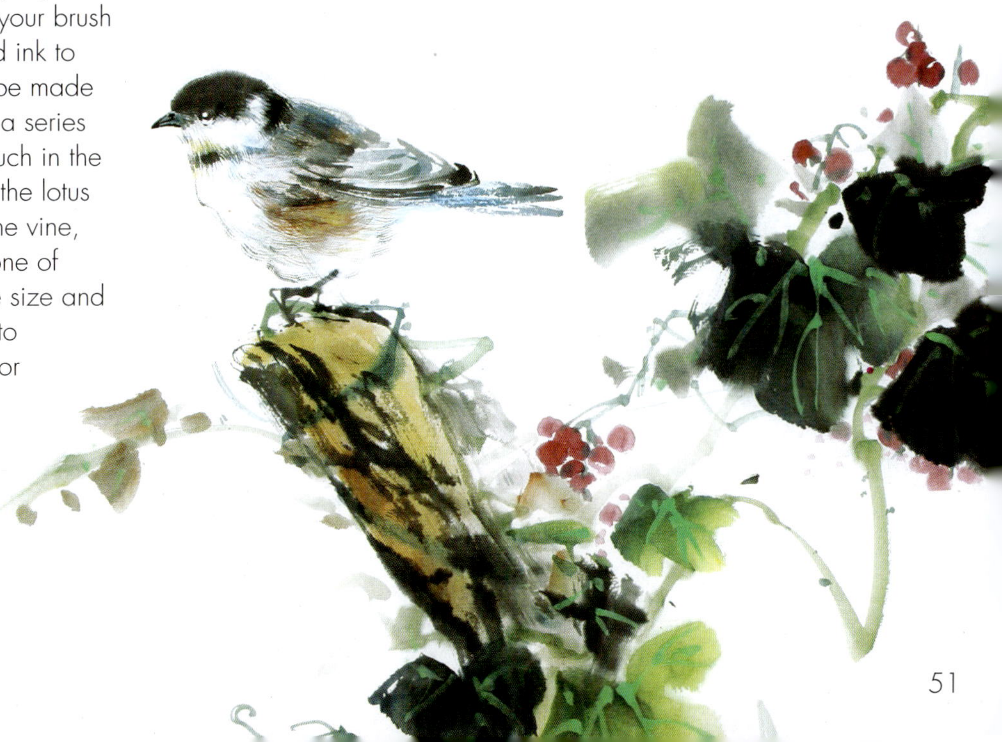

Great Blue Heron

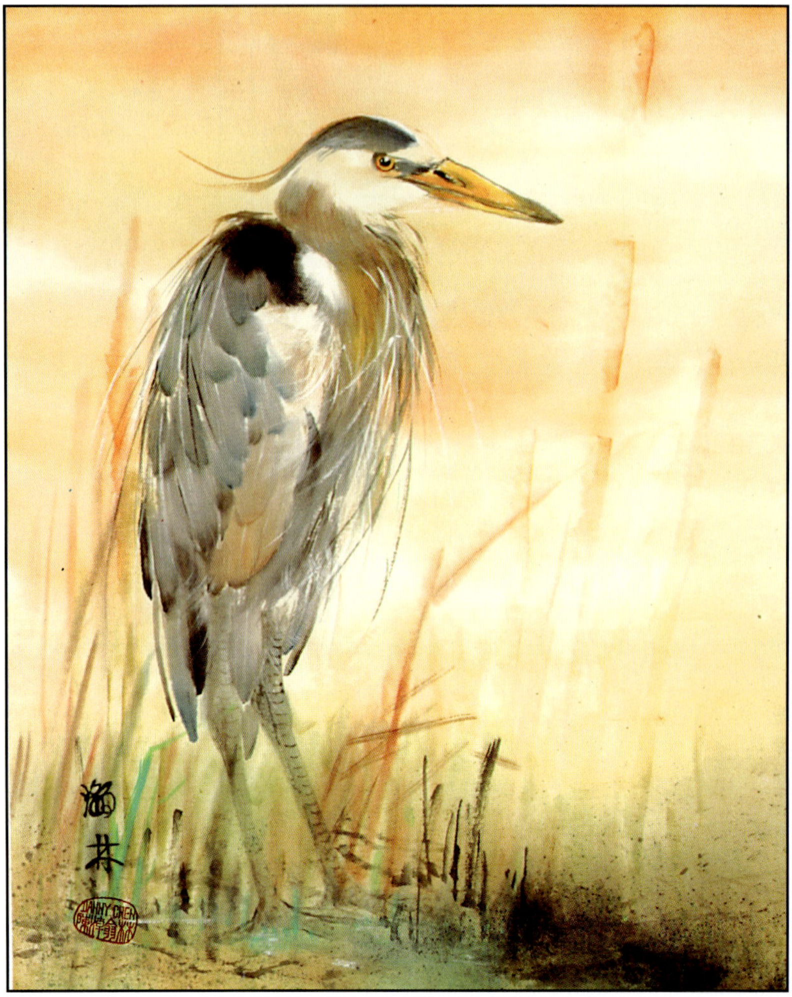

This painting of a great blue heron is not as complicated as it may first appear. As it is not as common a subject, there are fewer opportunities to study it in nature than the chickadee in the previous demonstration, but many of the brush strokes are simular. If you are in fact lucky enough to live where you can watch this bird in the wild, I encourage you to do so. I have also included a separate black and white sketch of the bird to guide your efforts in this demonstration (see page 62).

1.

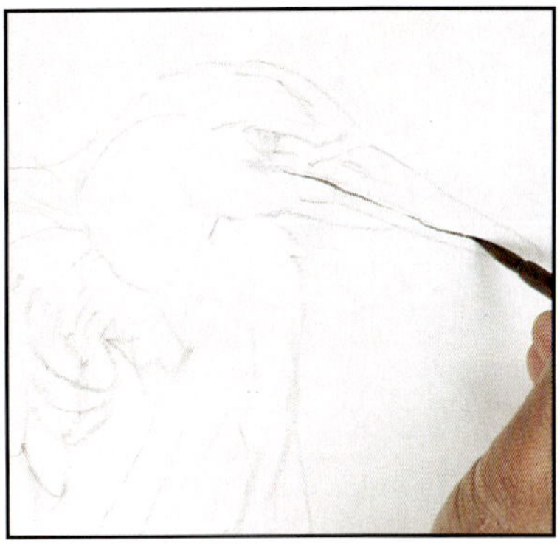

Begin with a sketch, tracing the image provided if you wish. Try making and using your own charcoal pencil from the tip below to do your sketch with, you will find it better to use than a traditional HB sketch pencil on xuan paper. Use your Vine brush and ink to trace over the outline of the heron. Work from the outside in, making sure that you capture form rather than detail at first.

2.

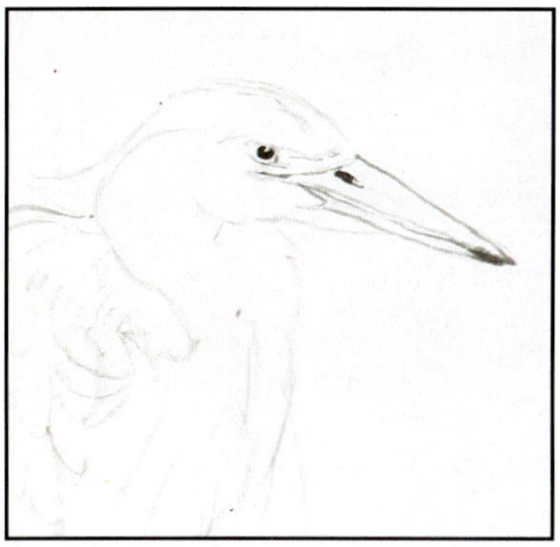

Keeping your fingers close to the head of your brush will enable you to control the movement of the brush better. Keep your hand in this position as you finish outlining the bird and then start to sketch the outline of the larger feathers.

3.

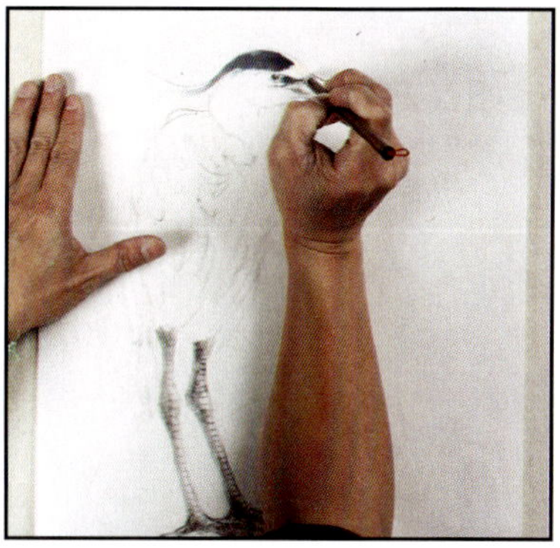

Once you have finished outlining the bird, use your White Cloud brush, and light ink to give the beak some shading. Next, load your brush and medium indigo and then with concentrated ink on the tip to paint the cap of the head with a single sweeping stroke. Start from the front and pull the stroke to the back adding wisps of feathers by lifting as you finish the stroke. Add a spot of color in the eye area with the same mix. Then mix concentrated white with a touch of burnt sienna to create a soft, creamy color. Spread the bristles of your brush and pick up a bit of this mix to fill in the white areas of the head. Use concentrated white to go back over these strokes with splayed bristles to stroke in feathery areas over the creamy areas.

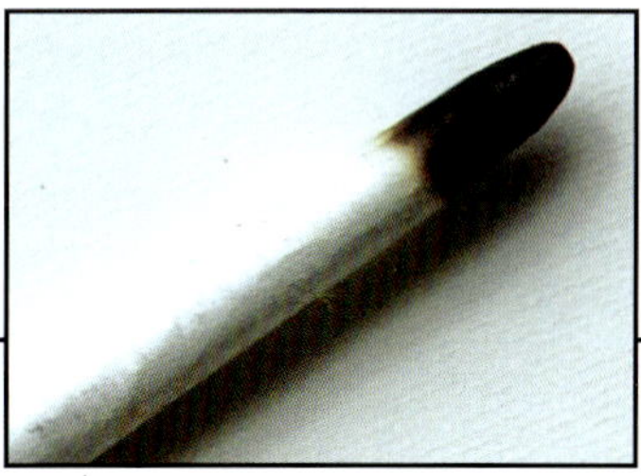

TIP

I use a homemade charcoal pencil for sketching because I find that a pencil, even a soft one is too harsh for xuan paper. Roll the xuan paper into a tight tube, securing it with a piece of tape, and carefully burn the end of it. The virtue of a homemade charcoal pencil is that the line it makes is very soft and there is almost always a scrap of xuan paper to use at your fingertips! Additionally, I am able to remove its mark by gently brushing at it with a feather or a very soft tissue leaving virtually no trace of it or damage to the paper.

4.

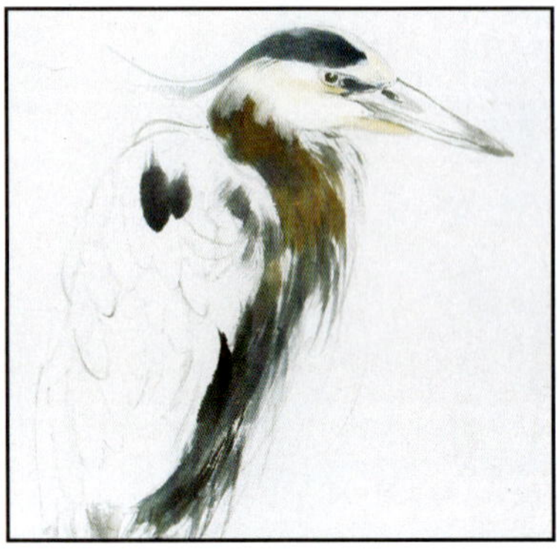

Mix indigo with burnt sienna to create a sepia tone. Using this mix loaded on your White Cloud brush with splayed bristles, add in the feathers around the chest and stomach. Reload your brush with sepia and then with indigo on the tip and continue adding feathers, lengthening the strokes as you work downwards.

5.

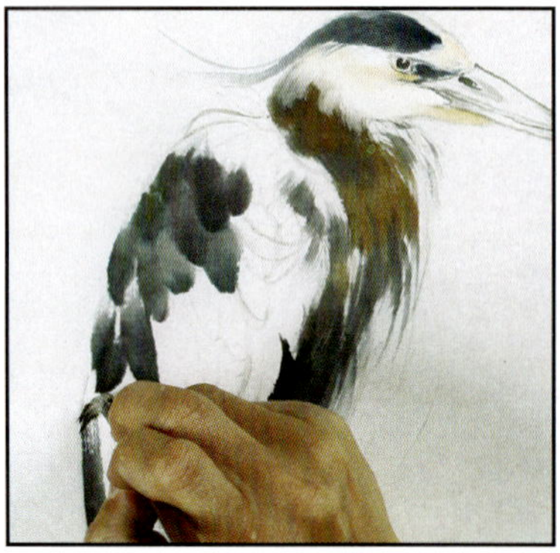

Paint in the wing next. Pick up indigo with medium ink on the tip and create each feather one at a time, with a single stroke pulled from the bottom of the feather to the top, lifting as you pull up to taper the stroke. Painting the feathers in this way will create the dark tip of each feather, graduating to the lighter top. Overlap the feathers as you go, working down the body. Follow the sketch as a guide to help you, noting that the feathers get longer and darker as you progress, so adjust the way you load your brush and the length of the stroke accordingly.

6.

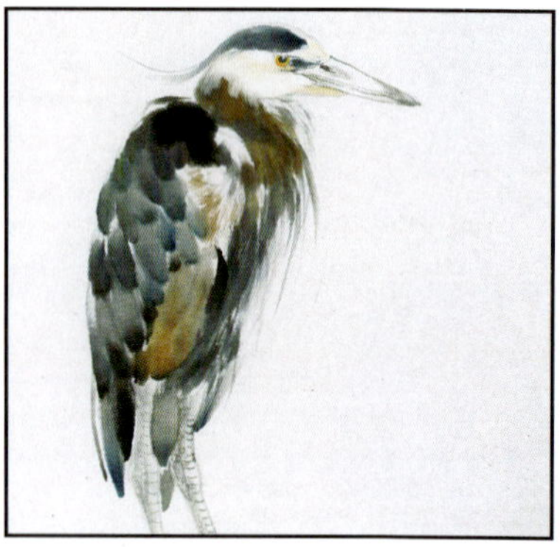

Finish the body of the heron by loading the whole brush with sepia and then adding concentrated ink at the tip. Again, referring back the picture, paint in the brown feathers by pulling each stroke upwards. Then, without loading the ink, very casually add in strokes around the neck area to create wispy feathers. Continue with your White Cloud brush picking up ink and splaying the bristles to do the dark patch on the shoulder. Next, with concentrated white and using the same technique, add in the white patches and a few long wispy feathers in the neck area. Next, using the Vine brush, pick up gamboge to color in the beak and eye. Finally, with your Vine brush and indigo, color in the leg of the heron.

7.

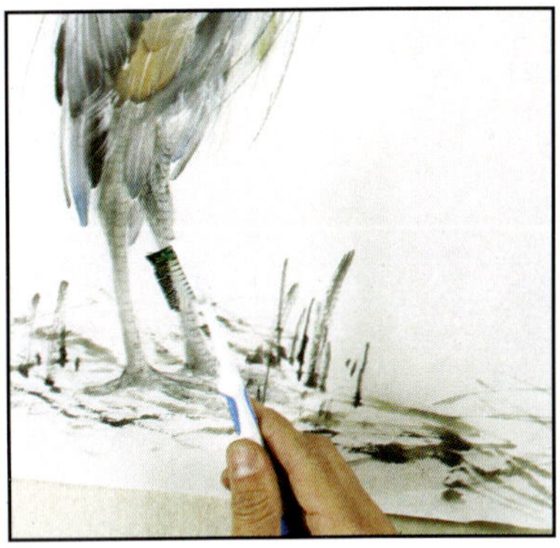

The heron is now finished and I am going to focus on the background. I start with the grass using my Orchid Bamboo brush. I use dark ink to start and progress to lighter ink using a dry brush stroke to create a look of dry grasses. Once I have the design in place, I use a toothbrush with ink and create a fine misty spray over the grasses. The first time you try this, you may want to cover the bird with pieces of paper so that you don't spray over the bird. With practice you will gain control over the intensity of the spray and the placement and won't need to do this. Once you have sprayed on the ink, then you can spray with a dark green as well. Let this spray dry completely in order to keep the colors from bleeding in the next step.

8.

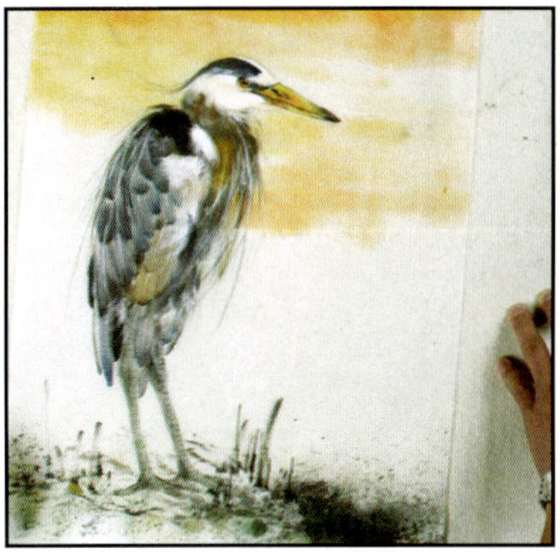

Your will apply a wash over the background now, which is why all of the previously painted areas must be dry; your don't want them to bleed. However, for the wash to bleed into the background and create a soft appearance, you must rewet the paper with a fine mist using a spray bottle. Using various tones of mixed orange and gamboge, paint in the background wash. You will notice that I let the background color go into the bird to give it even further color and depth and make it appear as though the color of the setting sun is reflected off of it.

9.

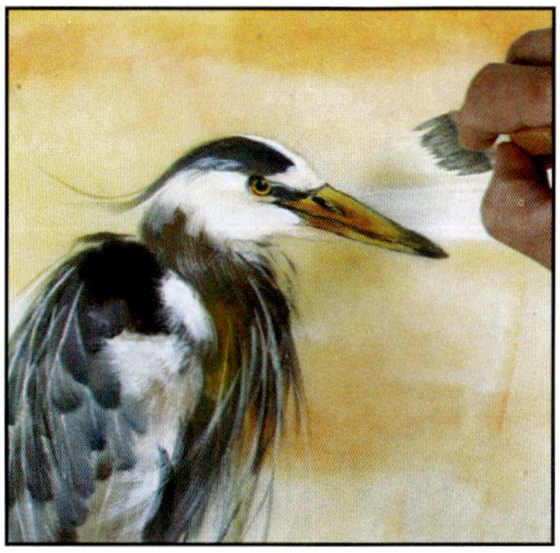

Work from the top of the page to the bottom, using lighter tones as you work down, and remember to keep remixing the colors as you did in the pumpkin exercise to achieve the rich tonal variation.While the background color is still wet, I added medium white with broad soft strokes to create a subtle, misty atmosphere. As a final touch, try scattering a bit of salt onto the background of your painting while it is still wet and watch what happens!

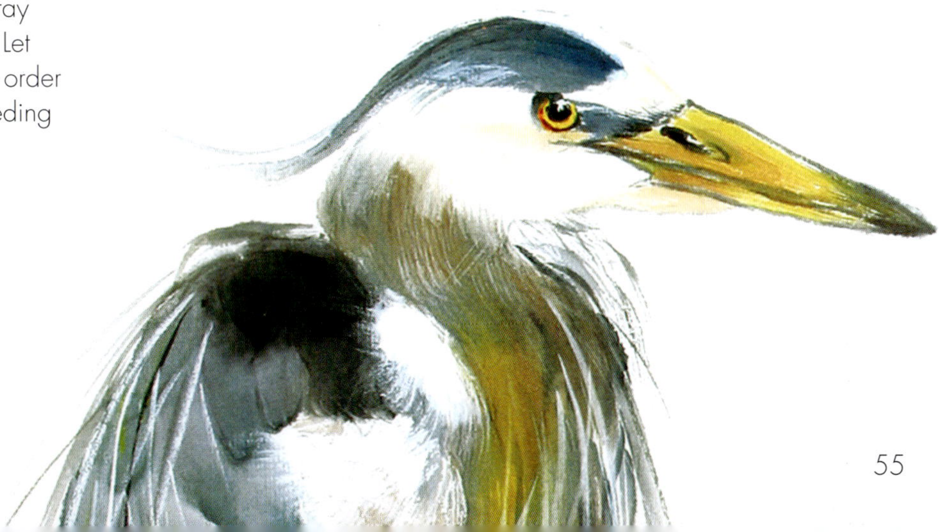

Goldfish

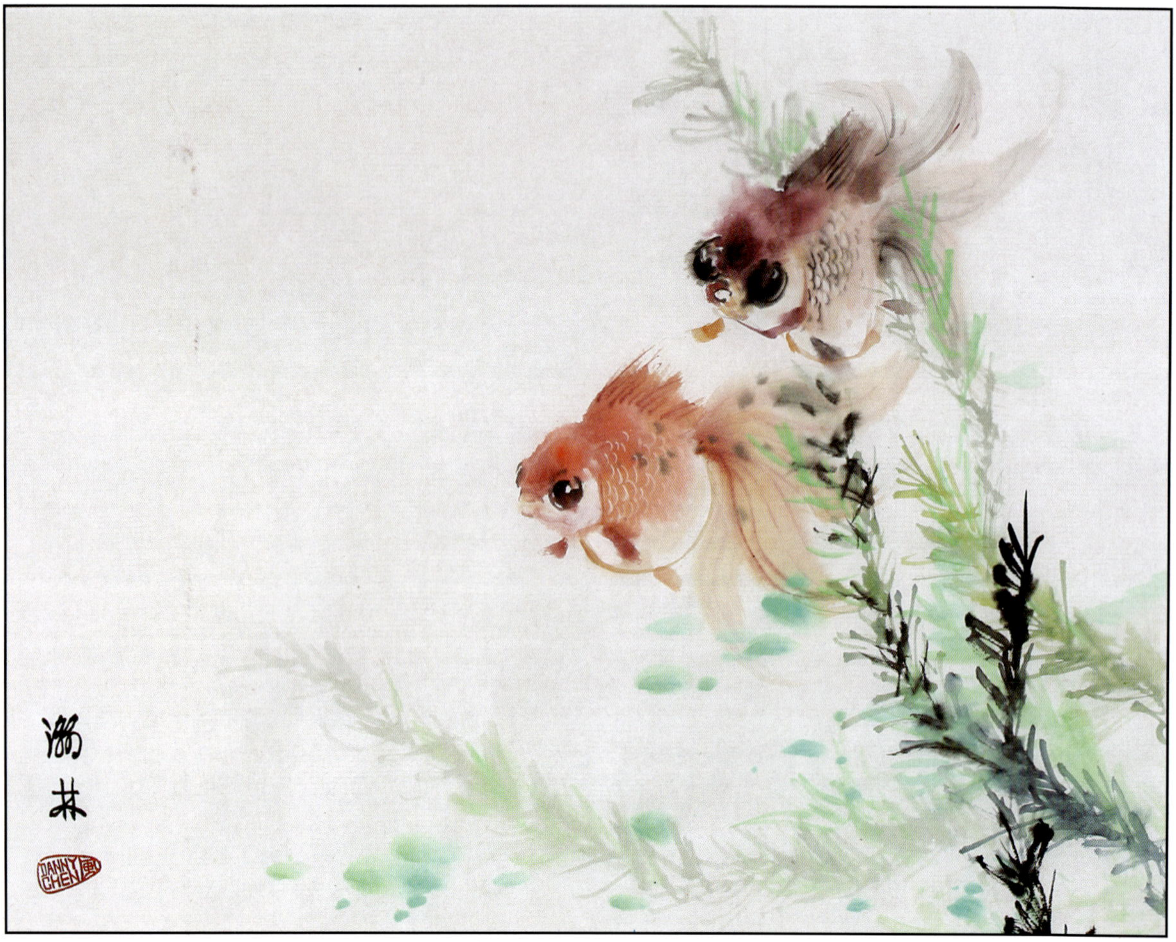

People enjoy painting this subject because the gold color of the fish represents prosperity and wealth in our culture. This is also a good *feng shui* subject and will bring good fortune to your home. Once you have completed your painting, be sure to hang it in an auspicious place in your house, such as in the entrance to welcome in good luck and prosperity.

1.

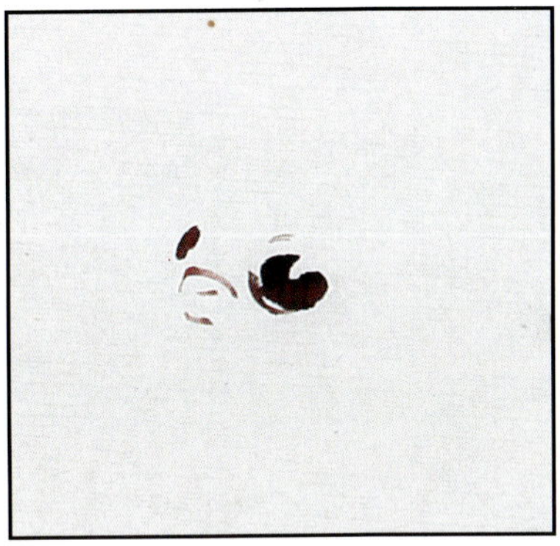

Use a Vine brush loaded with carmine mixed with ink to create the outline of the mouth and eye. Then reload the carmine and ink mix, loading the tip with concentrated ink to draw the circle of the eye, leaving a spot in the middle to reflect the light.

2.

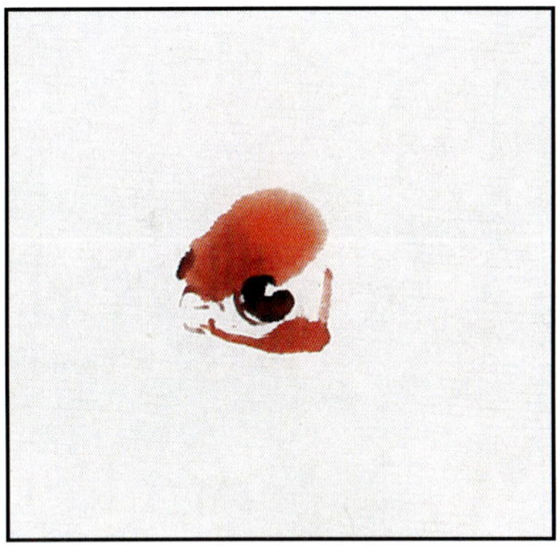

With the White Cloud brush, load mixed orange with carmine at the tip, and press down a small stroke between the eyes for the head. Reload the brush and paint in the gill area.

3.

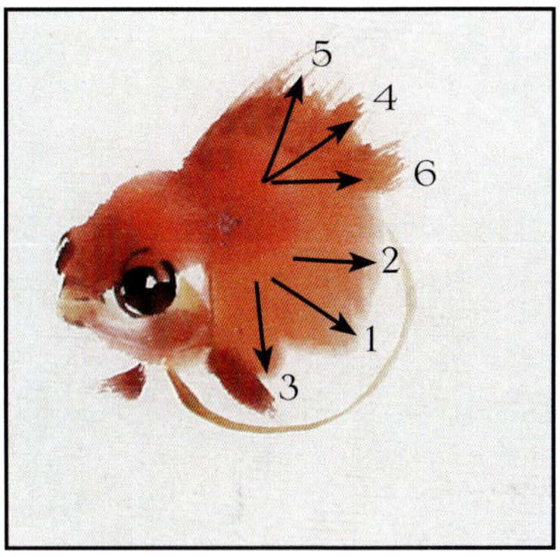

Reload the brush and fan out the bristles. Starting from the back of the head, pull out three strokes, one in the middle to start and then one on each side of the first stroke, pulling away with a side stroke. Then add in the dorsal fin. Reload the brush and holding it at a 45 degree angle from the paper, use three side strokes pulling up. Finally, add in the stomach. Reload your brush and make sure your bristles are in a point and add in a half circle starting from under the head and working to the back of the fish. Make sure it is a nice round stroke, you want your fish to be chubby and healthy! Add a pectoral fin with the White Cloud brush by adding two small strokes, pulling into the body.

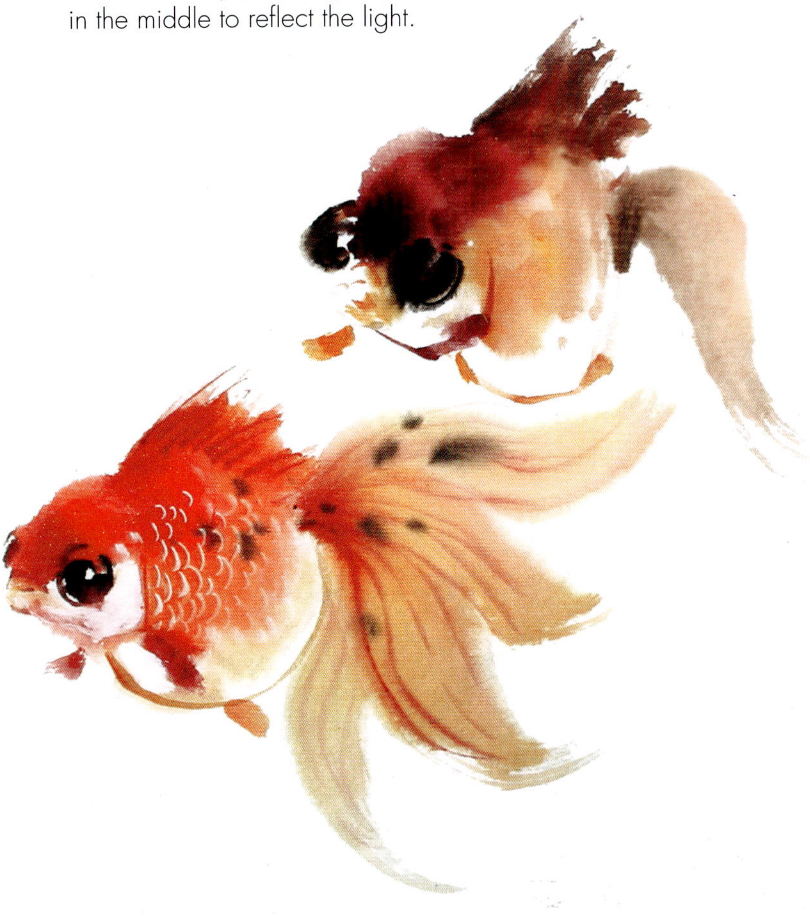

4.

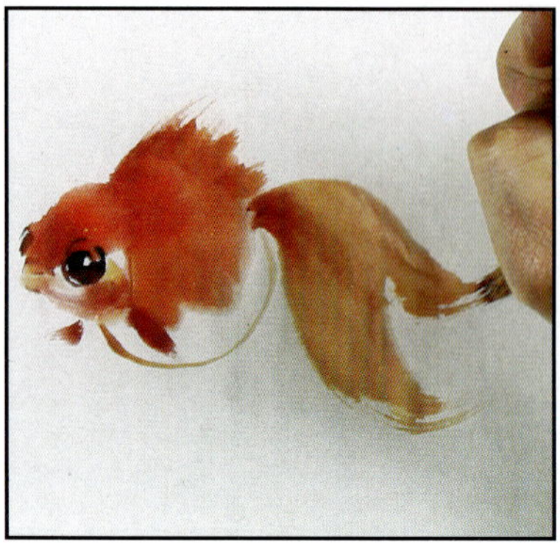

Use your White Cloud brush and pick up medium orange tipped with carmine. Start the tail by touching the tip of the bristles to the body and using a side stroke to pull out the first part of the tail. As you pull your brush, press down and to the side to create a squashed "S" shape, lifting at the very end to create the trailing wisps. Add two more strokes like this to complete a full, sweeping tail.

5.

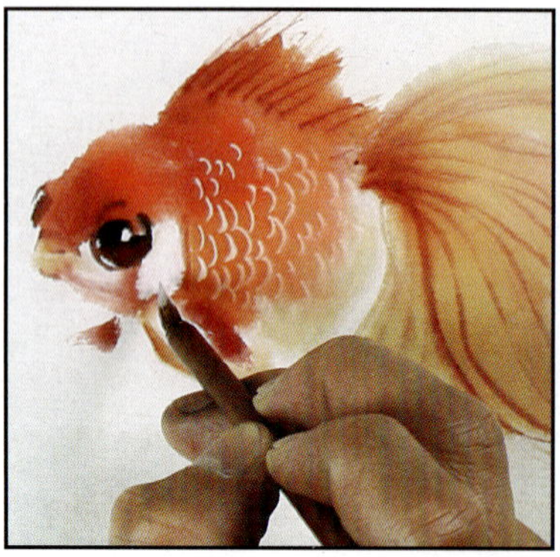

Load concentrated carmine onto your Vine brush and lightly add long sweeping detail strokes to the tail, and shorter, quick strokes to the dorsal fin. When you add these strokes to the tail, follow the lines of the tail to create a flowing sense of motion. Next, load your Vine brush with concentrated white and paint scales and a patch around the eye area, adding a highlight to the center of the eye if needed.

6.

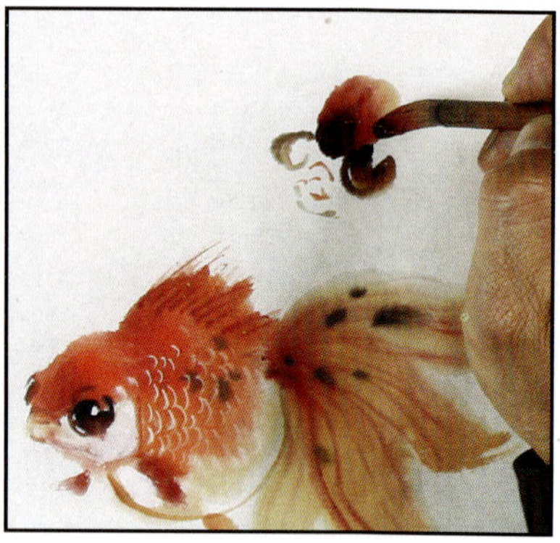

Finish with the White Cloud brush loaded with dark carmine, and casually dot the fish where you like to give it unique spotted markings. Proceed with the second fish using the same technique, but loading your Vine brush with ink for the outline. Load the White Cloud brush with dark carmine on the tip to press down the stroke between the eyes to do the head. Note that the stroke is in a more upwards position to reflect a more forward facing profile.

7.

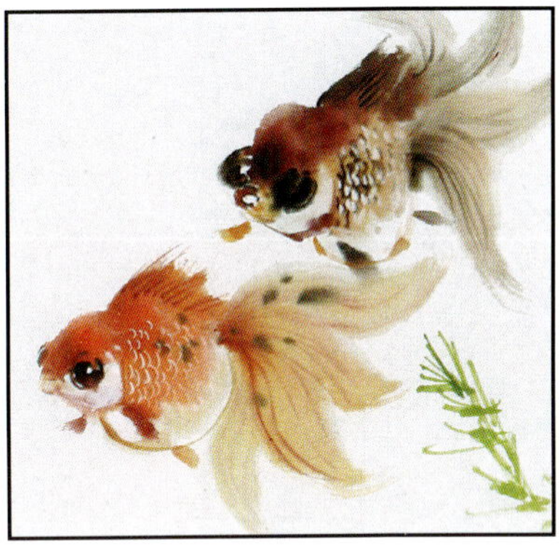

Finish the second goldfish using colors and markings that are lighter in tone. To do the seaweed use the Vine brush and pick up light green and dark green on the tip to give variation. To paint the plant traditionally, you would use a series of nail head rat's tail strokes, each one painted separately with a light feathery touch to create each individual leaf of the plant. I have created my own style of painting this type of a plant. It is fun and expressive, and gives a very "alive" feeling to the frond. Load your brush with your greens and start the plant at the top of the frond with a nail head rat's tail stroke but rather than lifting your brush off your paper at the end of the stroke, keep going and make dozens of short connects strokes. Let your brush go crazy!

8.

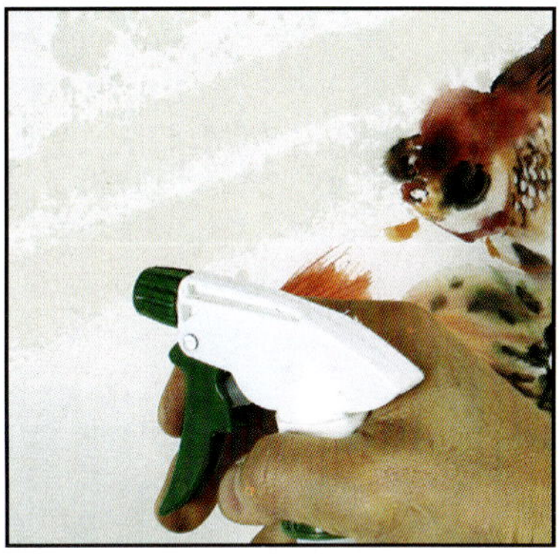

Make lots of back and forth strokes, working down the frond to the base of the plant without lifting your brush except to reload with paint as you need. This is a lighthearted way to quickly paint these plants and it creates a loose image full of movement. Practice doing this on your pad before adding a frond to you composition. Use your misting bottle to mist your paper and create random damp spots. Then, as you use opaque colors in a variety of greens, the dampness of the paper will cause your strokes to bleed more in spots. This will create a soft "watery" feel to the composition which is ideal for this subject.

9.

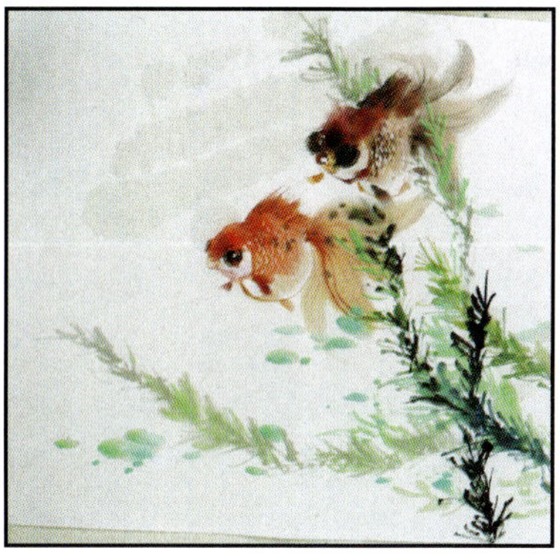

Finally, the water spots are created with an opaque green. Have fun with these spots and let them be water, bubbles, or whatever you want them to be. Remember that rules are made to be broken and let this composition be a reflection of how you see this subject.

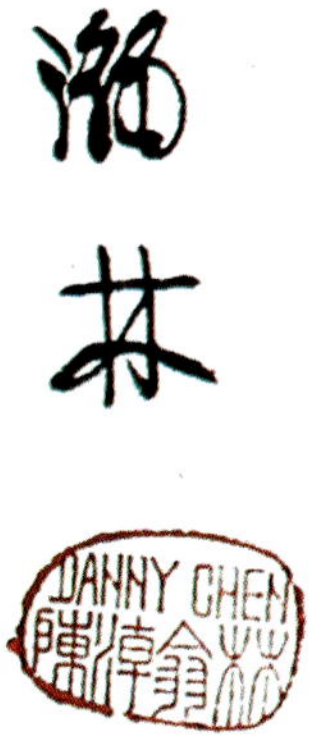

A Final Word from Danny Chen

Chinese art shares some similarity with Western watercolor, yet the techniques and material are quite different. Being a Chinese Brush painter with Western watercolor background in my earlier art career, I committed myself to develop the traditional Chinese painting technique into my own version of Contemporary Chinese brush painting. I have passion for promoting Chinese Brush painting, not only because of my cultural background as a Chinese, but because it is a wonderful experience to see that the beauty of a simple form can be built up within minutes on paper.

Regardless of your skill level as an artist I hope that this book has given you an opportunity to have fun using a brush loaded with colors, and has inspired you with all of the possibilities of Chinese Brush painting. A word of advice: after 25 years of teaching, I see that diligent practice is the only key to success in any style of painting!

I do encourage fellow artist and student who want to know more about Chinese painting to visit my website at www.chensgallery.com. You will see more samples of the subjects in this book as well as over 100 different pieces from my painting exhibit. You are welcomed to send me a picture of your work of the demonstrations in this book. We may even share your painting with other artists on our website!

I teach classes regularly at my studio in Richmond, B.C., Canada. I also host demo and workshops for private group or art organization throughout North America. Please contact my art team through email or my website for information about my workshops and classes.

ACKNOWLEDGEMENT

I have a great team helping me in administrating, marketing and promoting my arts through years. I would like to thank my wife, Hilda Yuet-Yi Chen, and my business manager, Linda Burchill, being my motivation and assistant in my art career; my parents and my very first art teacher, Mr. Huei-Tung Chen in Taiwan, being the inspiration of my art when I started at age 5; and most importantly, my art collectors and students throughout the world, who have been supporting me and encouraging me to be creative in my art.

Looking forward to your email sharing what you've learn from this book!

Warmest regards,
Danny Han-Lin Chen, AFCA

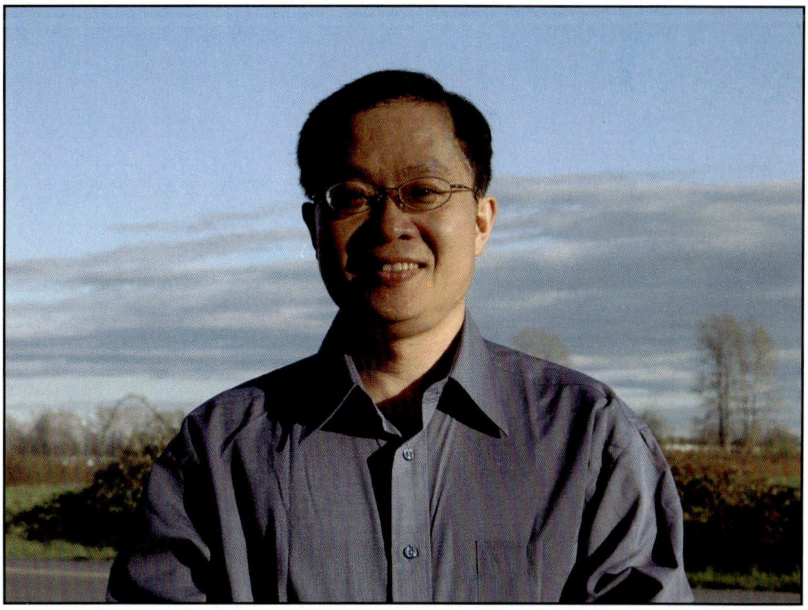

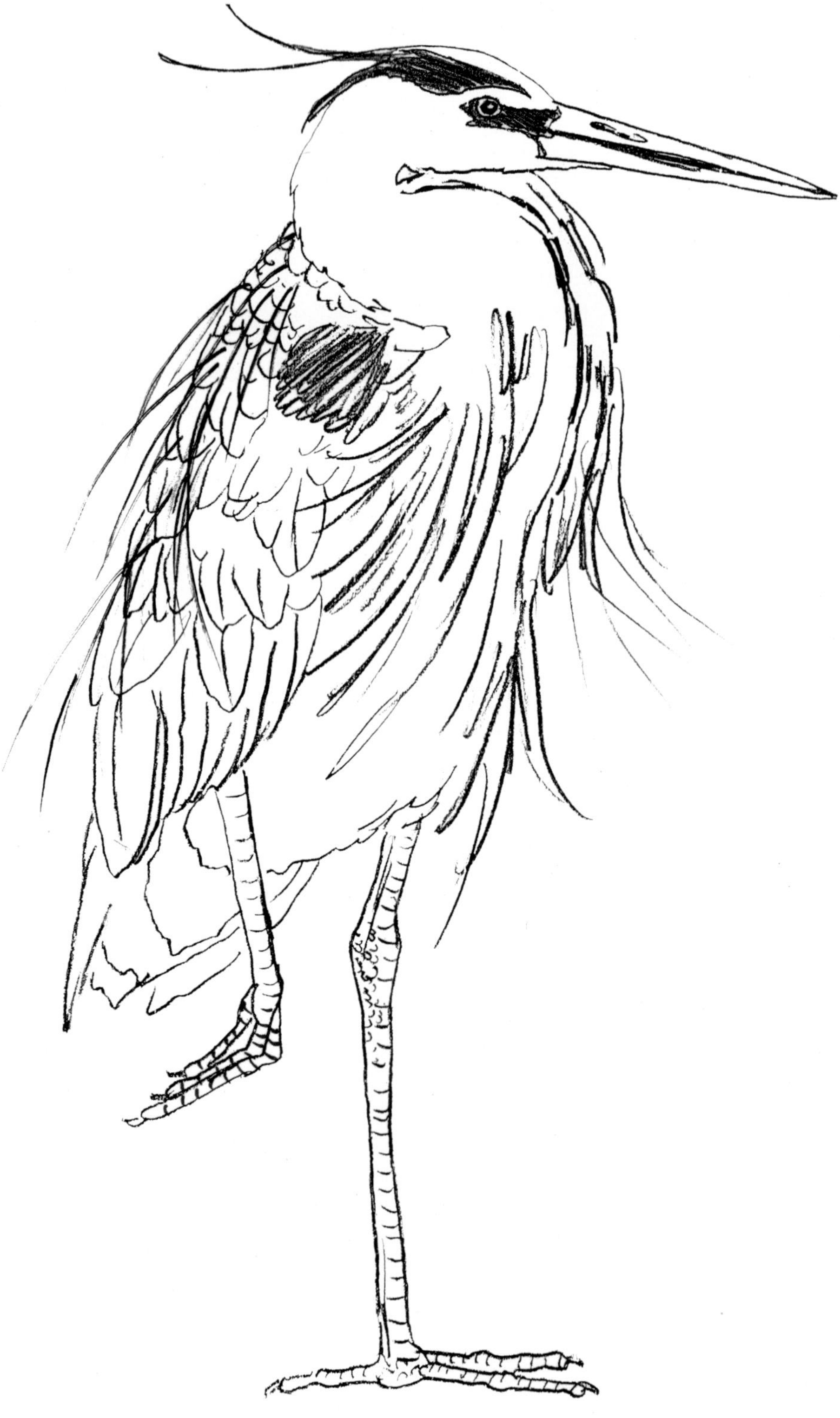

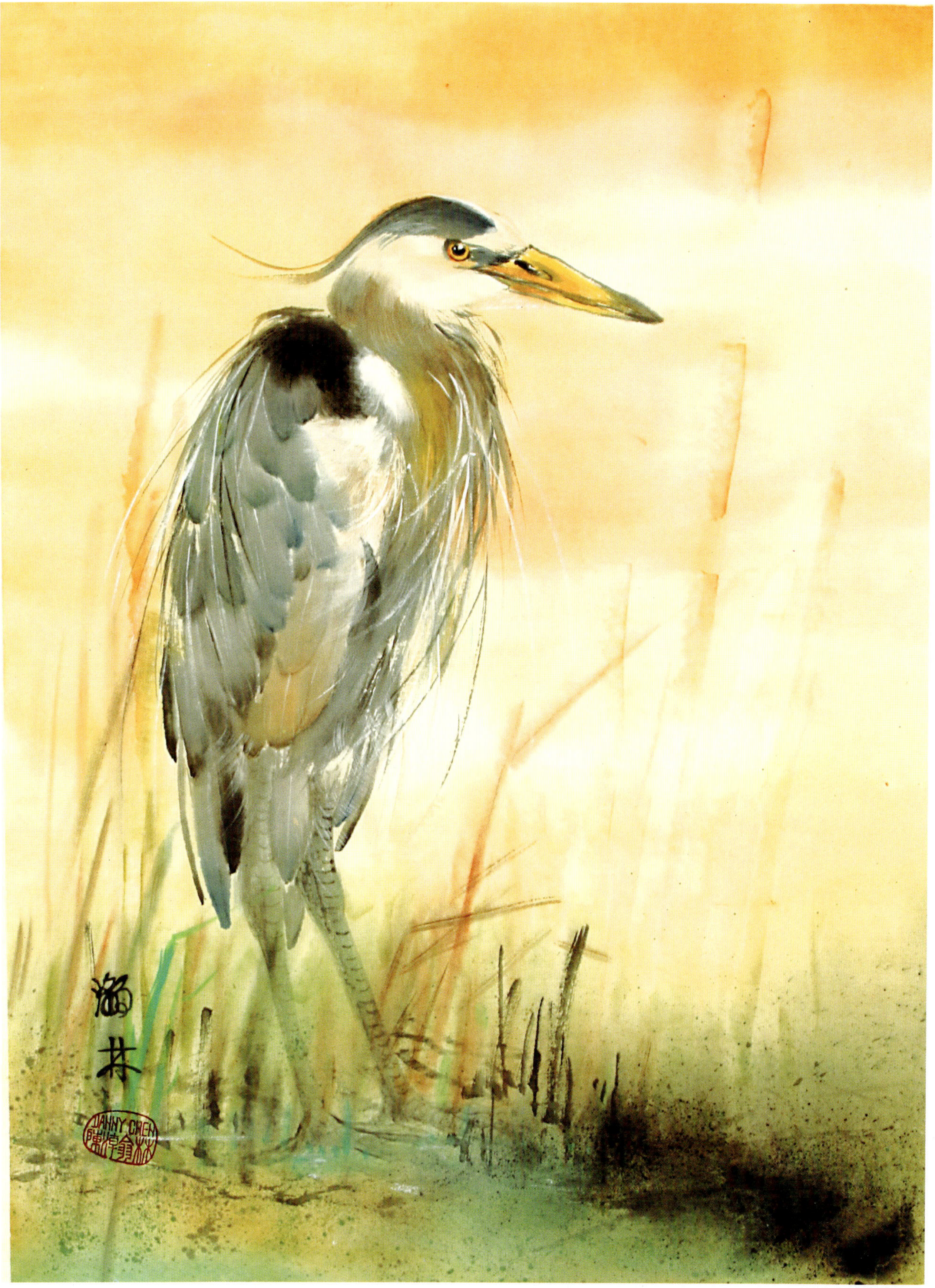
DANNY CHEN

瀚林

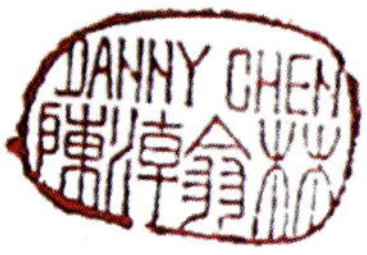